WILLARD BEAN

THE

FIGHTING PARSON

WILLARD BEAN

WILLARD BEAN

— THE —

FIGHTING PARSON

THE REBIRTH OF
MORMONISM IN PALMYRA

VICKI BEAN TOPLIFF

DIGITAL
LEGEND

ISBN: 978-1-937735-92-0

Digital Legend Press and Publishing

Salt Lake City, UT, and Rochester, NY

www.digitalegend.com

Send inquiries to: info@digitalegend.com or call 877-222-1960

Cover and interior designed by Jacob Frandsen

This book is dedicated to my children, Patricia, Julie, Michael, John, Jacqui, Jimmy, and Nikki, and to all generations that may follow that they may remember and appreciate the great heritage that is theirs.

CONTENTS

FOREWORD

Much has been written about Palmyra, the Sacred Grove and the Hill Cumorah in the early years of the Church. But what became of those historic sites after the Prophet Joseph Smith and his family left their small farm in upstate New York? The properties fell into the hands of non-Mormons who became increasingly more prejudiced and belligerent towards the Church.

The saints were driven out of their New York home in 1831. It wasn't until June 10, 1907, that Apostle George Albert Smith was able to purchase the farm for the sum of $16,000. Seven years later, he deeded the property to The Church of Jesus Christ of Latter-day Saints.

After gaining possession of the farm, the church authorities were faced with the task of finding a suitable family to occupy it. They needed a man, a fighting man, who could not only farm the land and care for the property but make friends and eventually converts in that hostile community. Those essential qualities were found in Willard Washington Bean, the seventh of ten children born to George Washington Bean and Elizabeth Baum.

The trials and experiences of the following 24 years are noteworthy as well as interesting and inspiring. The experiences that shaped the lives of Willard and his wife, Rebecca Peterson, prior to this call give insight into their growing testimonies and willingness to serve their Heavenly Father. These stories will be of special interest to their ancestors as they seek to learn more about their roots and will also serve to inspire and uplift and entertain all those who desire to learn more about the early history of the Mormon Church and the trials of the saints.

I have personally thrilled at the opportunity of doing this work. On many occasions as I have lingered in quiet moments researching and writing this story, I have felt the presence of these great ancestors by my side. I have felt their appreciation for my endeavors and hope that they feel the pride in me that I sincerely feel in them. When I meet them beyond the veil, I will know them and they will know me; and we will express a deep love and devotion for each other that perhaps cannot be felt in this earth life. I look forward to that moment.

Vicki Bean Topliff

PREFACE

Portraits of Significance . . .

Since the beginning of time it has been the natural desire of man to look up to someone . . . to admire someone to the extent that emulating them becomes instinctive.

In the beginning, of course, Adam, being acquainted only with his creators and those heavenly messengers who instructed him from time to time, had what we might term today "an easy time of it."

Yet, beginning with the earliest shepherds and continuing to these days of space pioneers, men and women have idealized others.

It is indeed difficult to conceive progress or perpetuation of any worthwhile endeavor without knowledge of men and women who have established patterns of living conducive to improving the quality of life and the desire to reach eternity with a clear conscience and no reservations.

Men and women of great character . . . staunch beliefs . . . great moral stature . . . selfless determination to serve God and their fellow men. These are those who are remembered in history, whose abilities and actions make them truly worthy of emulation. Just reading about them is an exhilarating experience. Even a chapter of their lives can change your life . . . make you glad you are part of the human race . . . stimulate you to greater accomplishments.

These are the characteristics which allow . . . no, cause men and women to shine forth, to light the way in a sometimes darkened world. These are Portraits of Excellence. These are my parents and my grandparents and those with whom they associated. Their spirituality has lighted the way for future generations.

I am proud to be a part of this great family, to have been raised by Willard and Rebecca Bean, to know Grandfather George Bean and Grandmother Elizabeth through their personal histories. I hope that you, too, will enjoy reading the following pages of the lives of the Bean family as much as my daughter, Vicki, has enjoyed writing them.

Alvin P. Bean

DEDICATION TO THE AUTHOR

Vicki Ann Bean Topliff
May 7, 1943–August 3, 2014

 Vicki is my sister. I say that with gratitude and pride. She exemplified purity, charity and love-the-Lord living all her life. An instant friend to all she met, Vicki welcomed many into her home and into her heart. She spent most of her adult life successfully raising her seven children, who then blessed her with 25 grandchildren.

As her children grew, Vicki was able to devote much of her time to writing books about our family history. She enjoyed being near the Family History Center in Salt Lake as well as the many resources available at university libraries for doing family history work. She spent many hours researching our family history through church archives of letters and other documents written by early church members to and from our grandfather Willard. Vicki loved writing and talking about our interesting family history, and gave many presentations to church groups about our beloved grandparents and their extraordinary contributions to the church.

In 2007, a ruptured appendix led to a rare and untreatable cancer which Vicki endured with remarkable courage and faith. One evening in 2014, while I sat with her in the hospital as she was nearing the final stages of her cancer, she pulled me close and spoke softly in my ear, "I don't want Grandpa to die with me. Will you carry on with the work I have done?" Surprised by her request and uncertain about my ability to succeed, yet eager to please her, I assured her I would be happy to.

With unmistakable Providential assistance, I am delighted that Vicki's books have now been professionally published in celebration of the 100th anniversary of Willard and Rebecca's mission call to Palmyra, New York, boyhood home of the Prophet Joseph Smith and birthplace of The Church of Jesus Christ of Latter-day Saints. These are stories that bind us together as family, and as members of the Church. Surely there is joyful celebration on the other side for this happy occasion!

I am honored to share Vicki's extraordinary gift of love with you, and thank Vicki from the depths of my heart for preserving our Palmyra legacy. She will be tenderly missed as her testimony, along with the testimonies of a long string of Beans, lives on.

With my deepest adoration and gratitude,

Lori Bean Henderson
Spring 2015

This photo was taken on Vicki's 71st birthday, May 7, 2014, three months before her passing. L–R: sister Lori, brother Bart, and Vicki.

THE VARIED CAREERS OF WILLARD BEAN

W illard Bean assumed many titles and as many roles throughout his picturesque life. As a small child, he was dubbed "Ka-pu-rats toats" (meaning "one-armed man's boy")[1] by the Indian children in Provo, Utah. During the mining boom in Goldfield, Nevada, many years later, he assumed the roles of Deputy Marshal and bodyguard. In religious circles, he was called Elder Bean or Reverend Bean; and in politics it was Mr. Bean. As a professional boxer, Willard was known first as Kid Bean and eventually The Fighting Parson.

Willard managed a gymnasium and sanitarium in San Francisco, California, which trained some of America's greatest pugilists. A newspaper article published in 1939 summed up not only his athletic character but the charisma and nobility he emanated throughout his entire life. It read:

> "Willard Bean won extraordinary acclaim as a boxer and physical trainer throughout the West. . . . He beat some of the best amateurs in the country and many of the crack professionals. Exceedingly rare prominence attended him in all his appearances because he never overlooked an opportunity, either by word or deed, to preach the gospel of clean living and good sportsmanship."[2]

1. Willard Washington Bean, Autobiography, p. 6, located in collection of Vicki Bean Topliff, Orem, Utah (hereafter cited as Bean, Autobiography).
2. Willard Washington Bean, Scrapbook, in possession of Barton Bean, Corona del Mar, California, and on microfilm in Brigham Young University Library, Provo, Utah (hereafter cited as Bean, Scrapbook).

THE FIGHTING PARSON

Early in his life, Willard grew to love the great outdoors. As soon as the winter snows melted, he habitually developed a pronounced case of spring fever and found it difficult to content himself in school. The rule in the Salt Lake Valley was to clear the fields of all livestock by April 1 which gave this anxious lad a perfect excuse to drop out of school and herd cows.

Willard's family owned a sawmill—the only industry in the county aside from farming and raising stock. When he grew big enough to pull one end of a cross-cut saw (lazysaw), he was drafted each spring to cut logs for the mill. Through this early exposure to physical labor as well as to the beauty of clean fresh air and the majestic mountains, Willard learned to appreciate the out-of-doors and spent the remainder of his life in active, physical pursuits.

Entertainment in the 1870s was mostly a program of self-improvisation. Willard and his friends found enjoyment in simple childhood games as well as competitive sports such as Big Boston, Knuckle Boston, three-hole perg, and the ever-enduring game of marbles. They also played skilly-vip, steal-sticks, spats-and-spurs, and many, many more. The boys made their own balls to play granny-up, granny-down, rounders, single-base, and double-base—the latter leading to the present-day game of baseball.

While yet in his teens, this budding young man began to show some promise as an athlete; but school athletics and sports were yet in their swaddling clothes. At summer resorts and on public holidays, Willard enjoyed watching the sprouting athletes display their skills in foot racing and wrestling. He delighted when the stuffed gloves were introduced, and ensuing years would see Willard excel in this new sport called boxing.

Before his 19th birthday, Willard was recommended as driver and camp caretaker for the Presiding Bishopric of The Church of Jesus Christ of Latter-day Saints (Mormon). These brethren had taken to traveling incognito in an effort to escape the federal government who had started a tirade against the men who embarked too freely on the sea of matrimony—otherwise known as polygamy. Hundreds had been arrested and confined to the penitentiary for five years or fined $500 or both. Willard left Richfield with the Presiding Bishopric on January 27, 1886, to accompany them on a lengthy journey to visit the members of the church in Mexico and outlying areas.

Willard's testimony was greatly enhanced as he traveled with these dedicated men of God. As they cooked around the campfire and rolled out their sleeping bags together at night, he learned much about the gospel of Jesus Christ and a protecting and loving Heavenly Father.

After traveling for over a year, enduring bitter cold during winter months and stifling heat waves at other times, Willard was received home with a hearty welcome. It was only a short time later that he received a letter from the Presiding Bishop asking him to take the mules, vehicles and camp equipment to Salt Lake City and deliver them to the barns on the Tithing Yard. During their extensive trip into Mexico, much of it over virgin territory, Willard was given a little money whenever he needed it; but no mention had been made of him actually receiving a salary. When he arrived in Salt Lake City, the Presiding Bishop handed him two tickets to an "Extravaganza Show" at the theater. It was the first BIG show Willard had ever attended. He was also presented with payment of $1.25 per day for his services. He felt like a budding millionaire. Being accustomed to having only store scrip and tithing scrip for services rendered in the past, the grateful recipient scarcely knew how to count real money.

The Presiding Bishop gave Willard a note of introduction to present to the manager at ZCMI Department Store telling him to let Willard have clothes at cost plus ten per cent. It was a thrilling new experience for him as he picked out a new suit with an extra pair of pants, shirts, and a new hat. When he arrived home, how he did strut!

THE FIGHTING PARSON

During the summer months, Willard returned to work at the sawmill thoroughly enjoying the fragrance of the pines, the wild mountain bloom, the wild berries, playful squirrels, and beautiful plumaged birds of the wide open spaces. When winter weather appeared on the scene, the mill was shut down; and Willard filled his spare time by playing minor parts in his home town dramatic company. He joined the Johnson-Houtz Company which was touring the state with a repertoire of three plays. Willard was assigned the comedy roles. On another occasion, he joined the Don-Either Dramatic Company reveling in his moments in front of a live audience.

In the spring, Willard and his brother, Burton, accepted the job of herding 750 head of church cattle. They were happy in their work and especially enjoyed the association with each other. At this same time, however, the Church found itself in legal entanglements. The Church was being sued by the government: "The Government of the United States vs. The Church of Jesus Christ of Latter-day Saints." The Church was convicted and was dissolved by the highest tribunal in the United States. Consequently, it did not officially exist for a time. Willard was summoned to Salt Lake City to meet Judge Zane to give an account of his stewardship. He lost his job, and the Church lost its cattle.

In 1890, at the age of 22, Willard was called on a mission to do ordinance work in the Manti Temple. He lived in the temple for two years assisting President Daniel H. Wells who was aging and needed constant care. Being young and athletic, Willard was a qualified font man and set a record which was probably never equaled. He performed 1100 baptisms for the dead without getting out of the font. As Willard dried off and changed his clothes that day, the temple workers encouraged him to "take the rest of the day off. Go get something to eat and then you rest. You've had a big day."[3] Willard had his dinner all right, but he had no intention of resting. Instead, he played baseball the remainder of the afternoon.

---

3. Rebecca P. Bean fireside address, October 1964. Tape recording and transcript in possession of Vicki Bean Topliff (hereafter cited as Bean tape recording).

THE VARIED CAREERS OF WILLARD BEAN

Willard was an avid baseball fan. A conference being held in Manti drew three men from outlying areas who also had a love for the sport. One such man, Neil Bradford, was an exponent of the curve ball. Willard and his cohorts arranged to meet the Fairview boys in a championship game Saturday afternoon following conference. Fairview had held the championship of Sanpete County for eight years. The scheduled game helped draw a large attendance at conference. The curve ball was new to the Fairview boys and dazzled them from the start. With Bradford in the pitcher's box, Bill Peas, a railroad ticket agent from Denver, on first base, Ab Murdock of Heber City as catcher, and Willard as shortstop, there was little the other boys could do to defend themselves. The fearsome foursome and their team won gloriously with a score of 12-0. During some innings, only the four "pros" even touched the ball.

Willard's tour of duty in the Manti Temple did not save him from full-time missionary service. He had scarcely been released from his temple duties when, on January 6, 1893, he received a letter from "Box B" asking him to accept a mission call to the Southern States. A local newspaper, The Richfield Reaper, ran this article as Willard prepared to depart:

> "Our athletic and amateur thespian citizen, Willard Bean, has been called on a mission to the Southern States, and those who are best acquainted with him will expect to hear of him going around the woods with a Bible under one arm and a set of boxing gloves under the other. He ought to be sent to Tennessee as it will take a fleet man to catch him and a good man to whip him when he gets hold of him."[4]

This turned out to be sort of a left-handed prophecy for Tennessee was exactly where Willard was sent. To make the call even more interesting, Willard was informed that he was going as a replacement for two missionaries who had been shot to death along with several Mormon sympathizers.

---

4. Bean, Autobiography, p. 26.

Following his missionary labors, Willard joined his brother, Orestes Utah Bean, in a play the latter had written called *Corianton*. Vaudeville and silent movies were just coming into prominence, and stage plays were beginning to fade. The entrepreneurs gained experience but lost $17,000. Willard later joined a Shakespearian company and toured the southern circuit as actor and stage manager.

Willard moved to New York and rented a room around the corner from a popular political campaigning spot on 96th Street. Being an admirer of Teddy Roosevelt, he wandered to that corner almost every evening to listen to the speeches.

The mode of operation was that each speaker would talk 25 to 30 minutes, drift to another stand and deliver a similar speech, then on to a third for his final address. One evening a large crowd had gathered, but the speaker, a state senator, was not in evidence. A mining engineer, who had spent considerable time in Utah and had seen Willard box, recognized him in the crowd and introduced him to the master of ceremonies. The two men convinced Willard to speak to the crowd in an effort to hold them until the senator arrived. Having caught the keynote address, Willard was able to expound eloquently adding flavor with his own verbose style. He struck a popular chord with the crowd and was drafted as a state bureau speaker.

A week later, Teddy Roosevelt was shot by a fanatical crank and orders were sent out to open future meetings with prayer pleading for his recovery. Willard, introduced as "Reverend Bean from the far west,"[5] was asked to pray one evening when the assigned minister neglected to show up. Later in that same meeting, he was asked to address the audience again in the absence of the scheduled speaker. Such praise was received following that oratory that Willard was promoted to a higher circuit and stumped in New York, New Jersey, Delaware and Maryland. One senator said if he could talk like Willard, he'd be the next president.

A Camden, New Jersey, newspaper wrote:

---

5. Ibid., p. 100.

". . .Willard Bean, an aggressive, convincing speaker from the far west, espoused the cause of Roosevelt. Every mention of Roosevelt brought a burst of applause."[6]

Occasionally a request would be made for a Christian man to speak. "Reverend Bean" was usually the man sent because on one occasion he had "quoted some appropriate scripture"[7] and impressed the religious element in attendance.

Willard engaged in one of the most profound missionary experiences in church history when he accepted the assignment by the First Presidency of the Church to move into the Joseph Smith home in Palmyra, New York. He arrived in that city on February 20, 1915, and sent for his wife the following month. Their instructions included breaking through the immense prejudice that existed there; making friends for the church and, eventually, converts; and purchasing historical sites of value to the Mormon Church.

Willard Bean successfully fulfilled this obligation before returning with his family to Salt Lake City, Utah, almost 25 years later.

6. Ibid., p. 101.
7. Ibid.

AN ACCOMPLISHED ATHLETE

W illard took part in a variety of athletic programs while attending Brigham Young Academy in Provo, Utah, in 1894. He excelled in many sports, but his real expertise was found in boxing.

When he asked permission to become a professional boxer, Willard's parents counseled: "You talk to the authorities about it. If they're willing, it's all right with us."[1]

With a genuine desire to continue in the sport yet be obedient to the counsel of the brethren, Willard approached the general authorities of the church. Their response was, "Ordinarily we would say no, but with the knowledge you have of the gospel and the friendly way you have about you, we think you would be able to do good by being a boxer. As you mingle with those people, and they see what kind of a life you lead. . .." Their response drifted into thoughtfulness. "You just go ahead," they concluded. "It will be all right."[2]

Willard trained for his sport with the diligence typical of his nature. Not surprisingly, he became one of the best. At the peak of his career, he became the middle-weight champion of the United States. Tex Rickard, owner of Goldfield, Nevada's, famous gambling hall and saloon and a man well-acquainted with the boxing

---

1. Bean tape recording.
2. Ibid.

game, was once heard to say, "The Parson here is the only man in Goldfield that gave the profession a tinge of respectability."[3]

In 1895, one of many newspaper articles written about Willard stated:

"He is 27 years of age, 5 feet 9 inches in height, and weighs in condition 154 pounds. His boxing contests have, with one exception, ended in his favor and usually by a clean knock-out. The one exception was a 22-round draw with Jim Williams of Salt Lake who was 23 pounds the heavier man. Bean is an ordained Elder of the Mormon Church and as a preacher has few equals. In his habits he is a model of correct living using neither tea, coffee, tobacco, nor strong drink of any kind, and since boyhood has studied along the lines of physical improvement. He has five gold medals won in the following competitions—hammer-throwing, shot putting, running, jumping, and boxing. On one occasion he took part, on a Friday evening, in a theatrical performance, as comedian. On Saturday he was one of the principals in a limited boxing bout, and on Sunday preached to a crowded house, all in the same building."[4]

Another article states:

"In each of his diverse professions (boxing and preaching) Bean excels. He talks eloquently and puts more persons to sleep by his punching than by his preaching. His discourses are celebrated in the church for their vigor and inspiration."[5]

After studying physical education and naturopathy in San Francisco, California, Willard returned to Salt Lake City, leased a sanitar-

---

3. Bean, Scrapbook (article written in 1936).
4. Ibid. (article written in 1895).
5. Ibid.

ium and started a gym where he taught boxing. One of his students was boxing great, Jack Dempsey, who remained a life-long friend.

"It was while I was running the gym that Dempsey, an awkward boy of 15, watched my instructions along with a gang of other lads," Willard related. "After I got through teaching, I'd take these young fellows and give them a bit of instruction.

"One day I matched Dempsey against a pretty good opponent. I saw he could stand up under punishment without flinching and that he would take a blow for the sake of giving a blow.

"Those were the days Dempsey wasn't getting 'three squares a day,' but he loved boxing. Well, I remember the day he said, 'That's the stuff for me.'"[6]

Twenty years later, Jack Dempsey hailed Willard as the "preacher" to whom he owed the success he was then enjoying.

George Albert Smith, one of Willard's early missionary companions in the southern states, had the pleasure of watching this gallant athlete in action. Three bullies approached the proselyting pair one afternoon as they were walking the streets of Tennessee.

"We're gonna beat the hell out of you," they boasted.

Willard replied, "Well, you'll allow us to fight back, won't you?"

The ruffians laughed. "Imagine preachers fightin' back! Course you can fight back," they bantered.[7]

Willard enjoyed a moment of ducking and floundering before landing a punch that sent one of the men into unconsciousness. Startled, the others stared at the inanimate body of their companion on the pavement then hastily fled.

---

6. Ibid.
7. Bean tape recording.

Willard's fighting ability played a significant role many years later as he walked down the flagrantly unfriendly streets of Palmyra, New York. A man watering his front lawn one afternoon turned the hose on Willard and said, "I understand you people believe in baptism by immersion." In the spry, athletic fashion to which he was accustomed, Willard hopped over the fence separating them and replied, "Yes, and we also believe in the laying on of hands."[8]

Willard was quoted often regarding his philosophies of physical and spiritual culture. His theory was this:

"When the body was entrusted to my care it was perfect in its organism. I am supposed to keep it free from all contamination; to keep it pure and undefiled; to uniformly develop all my faculties and all parts of my body to their highest capacity, that I may eventually bring my entire body to a symmetrical shape and the highest stage of development, approaching as nearly as possible that which God designed it, a perfect specimen of manhood in the image of my Maker, filling nature's measurements."[9]

8. Ibid.
9. Bean, Scrapbook.

A ZEALOUS MISSIONARY

Willard Receives the Call

Willard received a letter on December 9, 1892, asking him to accept a mission call to the Southern States. He had just returned from missionary service in the Manti Temple and found himself less than adequately prepared monetarily.

"I was all but financially broke, but I felt that I had no other justifiable excuse for my declining," he recorded. "By this time I had had enough gospel ground into me that I believed that by some means I would be able to scrape enough finances together to pay my fare to my destination and that the Lord would look after my needs while I was working for a good cause."[1]

A month later, on January 6, 1893, Willard reported at the office of the First Presidency and met President Wilford Woodruff. He was ordained to the office of a Seventy and set apart for his mission by George Reynolds.

Willard and ten other new missionaries assembled themselves in President Woodruff's office to get final instructions, arrange itineraries, and get tickets for their journey to Chattanooga, Tennessee. Willard, feeling the least qualified in the company, was placed in charge of the group with the responsibility of seeing that transfers were properly made and that the group arrived at mission headquarters in Chattanooga on schedule.

1. Bean, Autobiography, p. 26.

Salt Lake City, Dec. 9th 1892

Elder *Willard W. Bean*

Richfield.

Dear Brother:

Your name has been suggested and accepted as a Missionary to *the Southern States,*

The work of the Lord is progressing in the nations, and faithful, energetic Elders are needed in the ministry to promulgate the everlasting Gospel, openings for doing good appearing in numerous directions Yourself, with others, having been selected for this mission, should there be no reasonable obstacles to hinder you from going, we would be pleased to have you make your arrangements to start from this City at as early a date as *January 7th 1893,*

Please let us know, at your earliest convenience, what your feelings are with regard to this call. If you accept it you will receive no further notification, but will be expected to present yourself at the Historian's Office to be set apart on the day previous to that appointed for your departure.

Your Brother in the Gospel,

Wilford Woodruff

P. S. Please have your Bishop endorse your answer.

Willard Bean's mission call (above) and missionary certificate (right)

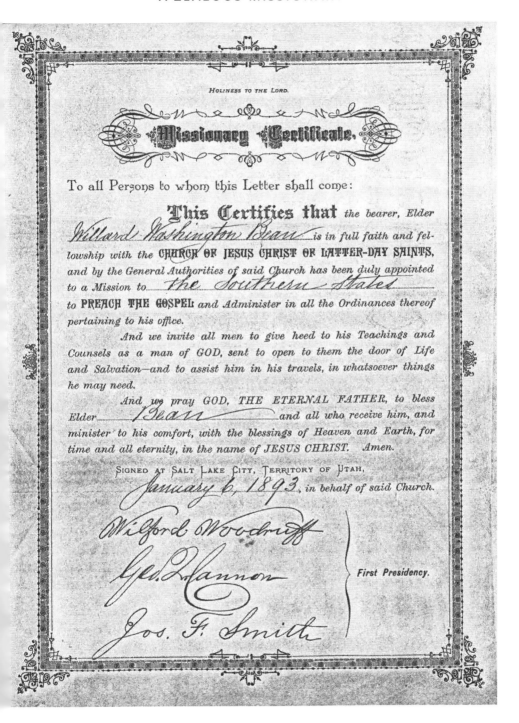

HOLINESS TO THE LORD.

Missionary Certificate.

To all Persons to whom this Letter shall come:

This Certifies that the bearer, Elder

Willard Washington Bean is in full faith and fellowship with the CHURCH OF JESUS CHRIST OF LATTER-DAY SAINTS, and by the General Authorities of said Church has been duly appointed to a Mission to *the Southern States* to PREACH THE GOSPEL and Administer in all the Ordinances thereof pertaining to his office.

And we invite all men to give heed to his Teachings and Counsels as a man of GOD, sent to open to them the door of Life and Salvation—and to assist him in his travels, in whatsoever things he may need.

And we pray GOD, THE ETERNAL FATHER, to bless Elder *Bean* and all who receive him, and minister to his comfort, with the blessings of Heaven and Earth, for time and all eternity, in the name of JESUS CHRIST. Amen.

SIGNED AT SALT LAKE CITY, TERRITORY OF UTAH, *January 6, 1893*, in behalf of said Church.

Wilford Woodruff

Geo. Q. Cannon

} First Presidency.

Jos. F. Smith

An Odd Companion

At that time in 1893, there were hundreds of young men who had never even seen a railroad train. Transportation had been either by horseback or team and wagon. One young missionary, arriving at the train station from cow and sheep country in the extreme section of Utah, gazed at the new mode of transportation in complete befuddlement. When the porter asked where he was going, he simply stated, "I'm goin' on a mission."[2] The porter directed him to Willard's car.

The young lad passed to the back of the car and took an empty seat. He carried a seamless grain bag with a strong string tied around the middle. Aware that one man was missing, Willard eyed the newcomer with interest. He tried to strike up a conversation with the lost soul but to no avail. Finally, he boldly stated that he and his companions were just starting for the Southern States on a mission.

The loner's reply was simply, "I haint got no valise."[3] Willard invited him to sit with the others but again came a cold and cautious response: "I'd ruther set here."[4] Each well-meaning missionary netted the same results.

As the men opened their bags and began eating, the "shipoke" in the rear of the car followed suit. When he untied his grain bag, his pie, cake, and bread and molasses were all jumbled together and resembled the mystery dressing in a Thanksgiving turkey.

J. Golden Kimball, president of the Southern States Mission, was out of the city when the new flock of missionaries arrived. George Albert Smith had just been called as mission secretary and had arranged for the group to stay at the Kennedy Hotel, "a very classy place."[5]

---

2. Ibid., p. 27.
3. Ibid.
4. Ibid.
5. Ibid.

The elders immediately went to their rooms to bathe and dress for dinner. Their "odd companion" had never worn a white shirt much less a clergy suit; and as he donned his new garb, he looked as if he had a board up his back and was trying to look over his collar.

Elder Smith instructed him to take his bag out the back way and empty the crumbled food. By so doing, he could put the clothes that were in the bottom of his bag in the new valise he had just purchased. Unfortunately, he only knew one way out of the hotel—and that was the way he had come in. He proceeded to take his grain bag through the hotel lobby and out on the front walk where he dumped the contents on the lawn in full view of the guests sitting in the lobby. He came back with the bag on his back and found himself faced with another agonizing problem. Which room was his? They all looked alike. One of the elders became aware that he had been missing for some time and went in search of him. He found the bewildered elder in the hallway trying door after door in search of the right one. He hadn't noticed that they all had different numbers on them.

When the missionaries went to the hotel dining room for dinner, their confused companion, having neglected to put on a coat, brought up the rear. Being an exceptionally formal hotel, a coat was required. The head waiter quickly spied him and informed him that he would have to be "fully dressed."[6] He didn't know what that meant, so the waiter got more specific and told him he must wear a coat. Another elder overhearing the conversation came to his rescue and escorted him back to his room in an effort to bail him out of yet another embarrassing predicament.

A Fighting Man

When President J. Golden Kimball met with Willard shortly after his arrival in February of 1893, he cautioned: "Elder Bean, you have been a fighter all your life. Things are different now. You

6.   Ibid., p. 28.

must turn the other cheek." Willard said he would be glad to turn the other cheek—if the guy could hit the first one![7]

George Albert Smith was Willard's first companion. This provided a welcome counterbalance. Two months after Willard arrived, however, Elder Smith was called to be mission secretary and Willard became a senior companion.

The elders traveled without purse or scrip. They walked from town to town and farm to farm tracting and hoping to be invited into the homes to preach the gospel. Many times they went without food and slept on the ground in the woods. They prayed several times a day and relied on the Lord to help them.

News of Mormon missionaries being in the vicinity always preceded them, and often they would see notices tacked onto trees beside the road warning them to leave the county or be killed.

Willard was not easily persuaded to leave. His reaction was courageous as well as unconventional. He tacked notices on top of the others announcing the elders' intention to preach Mormonism to all who would listen and stating their willingness to debate with anyone on any religious subject at any time and at any place.

Many of the notices posted by townspeople were bluffs—but some were not. One hot day the elders entered a town and, walking up to the central square, asked for a drink of water. Having already been recognized by their clergy suits, they were refused. Undaunted, Willard began to preach and pass out tracts.

The town bully and leader of the mob, standing 6'6" tall and weighing 230 pounds, stepped out and said, "Men, if we strap these preachers across a log and whip them with hickory withes, they'll remember us a long time."

Willard replied, "Let's make this a sporting deal—just you and me. If I lick you, we preach. If you lick me, you get to whip us."

---

7.   "Willard Washington Bean, Mission in Tennessee 1892-1894." Talk given by Alvin P. Bean. Transcript in possession of Vicki Bean Topliff (hereafter cited as Bean, Mission).

With haughty confidence, the big brute accepted the challenge. It was a typical David and Goliath battle. Willard laid his Bible and Book of Mormon on a stump saying, "Lay there, religion, while I prepare this man for Mormonism." The result was inevitable. Willard's boxing prowess led him to an easy victory. The townspeople gained respect and a renewed fascination for these "men of the cloth," and the elders were offered the schoolhouse to preach in as often and as long as they wished.

"And me and my boys will see that it's packed every night," announced the defeated but amicable competitor.[8]

On another occasion, Willard and his companion came upon a group of picnickers in the woods near Possum Gulch. Running and jumping contests were part of the festivities—and Willard was a pro. The elders began to introduce themselves when one over-zealous hillbilly jumped to his feet and said, "You'll do no preachin' here as long as I can stand on two legs."

Willard said, "Well, now, that's okay. And while you're on your back, I'd like to show you how we run and jump and tumble in Utah."[9]

Yes, when the dust cleared, the clergy suit was a mite soiled but still upright. Willard proceeded to put on a tumbling and acrobatic show. He beat their best broad jumper by two feet and jumped a team of horses without touching a hair.

One man observed, "You're the fightin'est preacher we ever saw in these parts."[10]

Within a year, seven families from the picnic had been baptized.

On another occasion, a Brother Watson told the story that he witnessed a mob tying Elder Bean to a tree intending to beat him with hickory withes. While stripping the clothing off his back, Elder Bean said: "You are a bunch of cowards. You tie a man up so

8. Ibid., p. 2.
9. Ibid., p. 3.
10. Ibid.

he can't defend himself. If you'll let me loose, I'll take you on two at a time and whip the whole bunch of you!"

The mob snarled and laughed and untied him. Two of the leaders made a lunge for Willard and were flattened in seconds, and he disposed of four others just as quickly. No one else cared to expose his face to the elder's seemingly iron fists. That elder had the power of Sampson that day, noted Brother Watson.

Then Elder Bean said to the mobsters: "Don't run off now. Sit down and let me show you that I can preach even better than I can fight."

"He could and he did," said Brother Watson. "I was on the fringe of that mob that day. I heard and saw it all and was converted by that sermon."

Another report tells of Willard traveling alone through the East Tennessee woods one day, walking through dust and mud with his toes sticking out of his shoes. He came upon a group of men attempting to shear sheep. They had some 20 or so unsheared sheep waiting in a pen. They had one on its back, all four feet tied together, and they were struggling to get the job done. Willard, after watching in amusement for ten minutes or so, said to the men: "If you will pass the hat and get enough money to buy me a pair of shoes, I will shear the rest of your sheep and have it done in less than an hour."

Willard had come from sheep country where a dozen men would shear a thousand sheep a day. They would have contests to see who could shear a sheep in one minute's time—and this with old hand-operated blades.

Money was collected—enough to buy shoes plus a hat. "But," said the man collecting the funds, "we won't give any of it to you if you fail to do it in less than an hour."

Willard did not fail, and he received his pay. He then announced himself as a Mormon Elder and said he would like to prove himself a better preacher than a sheep shearer. He must have proven it for, as the story was told, half that group eventually joined the church.

Willard took advantage of every opportunity to make friends, which, in turn, led to conversions. Soon the warning notices on the trees changed to invitations beckoning him and his companions to come to various homes or schoolhouses to preach. People would come from miles around on foot, horseback, buggies, wagons, even ox cart, to hear the elders expound the gospel of Jesus Christ. Willard debated with many professional anti-Mormon lecturers. One was converted! Another, though not converted, stood up after Willard's rebuttal and promised the audience that he would never again lecture or say anything derogatory against the Mormon faith.

Willard's ability to quote scripture from memory impressed the southern people immediately. Heber J. Grant said on one occasion that he knew no man in the church who could quote as much scripture as Willard Bean.

The townspeople developed a kinship for Willard as they watched him play on local ball teams and accompany band concerts on the snare drum. One minister who said, "They'll preach in this town over my dead body," was right. He died four days later, and the elders literally preached over his dead body.[11]

Many posses were formed to kill the missionaries. Posses were counter-formed to stop them. The Silver Hill Gang protected the elders against the Walker Hill Gang. There was no end to the danger and excitement in the lives of these early missionaries.

Conversions were numerous. Friends multiplied and even enemies were forced to laud Willard as the "preachin'est feller to ever hit Tennessee."[12]

11. Ibid., p. 4.
12. Ibid.

A Lame Friend

Willard and his companions spent much time tracting and proselyting in Putnam County. Being the senior elder and observing that they had "worn the grass off and that it was time to change pastures," he suggested to his companion that they pack their bags and head for "we knew not where."[13]

They soon found themselves in White County and learned that they were in virgin territory as far as Mormons were concerned. They were surprised and disappointed at the cold reception they received. Many people even refused to accept tracts. As time went on, they became more calloused to rebuffs and insults. They gained confidence in themselves by the hour. Prejudice became more pronounced, they observed, as they neared Sparta, the county seat.

As the elders tracted about three miles outside of Sparta, they noticed a lame man at the side of the road. After engaging in conversation for a few minutes, the man, who introduced himself as Ramsey, became interested in the Mormons and suggested that the elders hold a meeting near his home. He was the custodian and caretaker of a schoolhouse which doubled as a chapel, and he volunteered to escort the missionaries to meet with the trustees to ask permission to preach in their building. Willard was told that the Campbellites met there regularly every Sunday morning, but that other denominations frequently preached there starting their meetings right after the Campbellite Sunday School services concluded.

Two of the three trustees readily gave their permission for the Mormon elders to preach in their schoolhouse. The third requested time to consider it. While he was contemplating the issue, the elders took opportunity to tract in the area of the school. They became aware of considerable contention between the Campbellites and the Presbyterians and Methodists—and all of them prejudiced against the Mormons.

13. Bean, Autobiography, p. 29.

As darkness approached, the elders sought lodging. Home after home turned a deaf ear. An oft-heard response from the Campbellites was, "Sorry for you all, but we all are Christians here."[14]

The pair continued seeking shelter until no more lighted homes could be seen. They headed into the woods, knelt in prayer, then assembled enough oak leaves to make a soft pallet and curled up for the night.

The next morning was Sunday. They left their makeshift sleeping quarters in the woods and made their way to the little schoolhouse-chapel. While sprucing up for the Sunday services, they were spied by their new friend, Ramsey. He became suspicious and inquired where they had stayed the night before. The elders evaded the question and endeavored to change the subject. Ramsey then asked if and where they had eaten breakfast. The elders were on the spot. They replied that it was not uncommon for missionaries to fast Sunday morning "to give the spiritual the ascendancy of the physical."[15]

"I can guess the rest," Ramsey replied. "You can't fool me. You're going to eat some breakfast. Come with me."[16]

In a predictably gracious manner, Ramsey escorted them to his home. His wife was in poor health but had a big heart and welcomed them warmly into their family circle.

The elders attended their Sabbath School and were introduced to Professor John Nowlin. At the close of their exercises, the professor announced that the Mormon elders would hold a meeting and invited the people to remain. Professor Nowlin announced further that he had been informed that the missionaries had slept in the woods in a Christian community and expressed his profound regrets. Willard and his companion had made it a matter of prayer before leaving the woods and beseeched the Lord to assist them in their meeting that good might result. The Lord did not dis-

14. Ibid., p. 30.
15. Ibid.
16. Ibid.

appoint them. "We preached better than we knew,"[17] was Willard's comment reflecting on the meeting. Their sermon brought tears to the eyes of many who were present, including Professor Nowlin.

Many members of the congregation stopped to ask questions following the meeting. Others extended a warm handshake inviting the elders to call on them. Professor Nowlin and his wife invited them to their home for dinner and to spend the night. The Ramsey family joined them for the evening, and all expressed a desire to know about the gospel. Both missionaries were "green," but not infrequently the Lord magnifies the weak things of the earth to confound and convince the wise. The elders explained that some of the early converts to the church were disciples of Alexander Campbell who, when they heard the gospel in its fullness, accepted it and became apostles in The Church of Jesus Christ of Latter-day Saints. Their small audience became deeply interested, and Professor Nowlin could readily see where his own religion was lacking.

The professor had been state senator and at that time was county clerk. He extended a standing invitation to the elders to call on his family any time they were passing his way and to use his office to read and answer their mail. He and his family were baptized and later went to Utah where Professor Nowlin taught Latin at the church university.

Reverend Bowles' Malicious Plan

The next day, Willard and his companion headed south venturing into new territory. They crossed over the Caneyfork River into DeKalb County where they spent the night with a well-to-do Campbellite family having considerable influence in the community. The elders readily accepted the offer to preach in their chapel the following Sunday.

The next several days were spent in tracting and advertising their upcoming meeting. They were pleasantly surprised at the

17. Ibid.

large congregation that assembled that Sunday morning. "Jesus, Lover of My Soul" proved to be a perfect choice for an opening hymn as most of those present were familiar with that song. The audience sang with gusto. Willard's companion offered a few opening remarks, and Willard gave the concluding sermon.

After the benediction, the people gave no indication of being ready to depart. The reason became apparent in only a few moments as a burly-looking man in ministerial garb hastened to the stand and waved the people to remain seated shouting aloud, "I am going to take Joe Smith's Mormonism by the topknot and puncture it so full of holes you can see daylight through it."[18]

He opened his knapsack and took out two or three fiction books on Mormonism. What a villainous tirade followed, and his personal accusations were even more vitriolic and venomous. But his plan backfired. Some in the congregation cried out, "Shame, shame," and got up and left the chapel.[19]

The Campbellite family which had entertained the missionaries so splendidly the night before took them home again and apologized for the abuse they had suffered. He assured them that the preacher, Reverend Bowles, was not invited and had, in fact, canceled another appointment to preach just so he could be in attendance and antagonize the Mormon elders. Reverend Bowles made enemies with his little tirade, whereas the missionaries had the sympathy of the congregation and made many friends.

Another Cold Reception

Willard and his companion started back to Boma, Putnam County, to stock up on literature and get some washing done, etc. As they journeyed along the bank of Mine Lick Creek, they spied four men sitting on the front stoop whittling and spitting tobacco juice into the dirt. One of the men got up and went into the rural store which also served as a post office. Presently a man came out

18. Ibid., p. 31.
19. Ibid.

whom they later learned was the owner of the store, postmaster and justice of the peace. He was in his shirt sleeves and was bare-headed. A pistol dangled in his hand. As he approached, the elders sensed trouble as he looked red hot about the gills. His salutation was simple and to the point:

"What the hell are you damn Mormons doing back here? Haint we told you to never come back here again? Didn't we tell you that if you showed up here again we'd fill yer hide so full of holes it wouldn't hold taller? And when we say a thing, we mean just that."[20]

When Willard got a chance to speak, he explained that they were strangers in the community and had only been in the state a short time. He suggested that if their presence was obnoxious to the people in that town that they would change their base.

The belligerent intruder concluded with, "If this is your first visit to these parts, let it be your last. There's the way to Boma," he said, pointing. "Now keep goin'."[21]

The elders sauntered on along the creek confiding that if their mission experience continued in the same vein as the first two weeks, they would have a heap of experience before they got home. They decided to take these things in stride and continued confidently down the road.

A Picnic Exhibition

After a two-mile walk down the creek, the elders heard music coming from a nearby grove of trees. Their path led them over a high foot bridge and into the grove. As they neared the clearing, they saw a small group of men jumping. When the men caught sight of them, they had no trouble classifying them by their ministerial attire. The picnickers went into a huddle.

---

20. Ibid., p. 32.
21. Ibid.

A ZEALOUS MISSIONARY

As the elders neared the group, they were stopped right where the jumping had taken place. Willard happened to be by their jumping mark and casually looked to determine the distance made by their jumps. They had been jumping hop, step and jump, or two hops and a jump. As he stood by the starting mark, an old gentleman, their rural blacksmith, shouted in a shrill voice: "Get out of the way and let's see him jump, damn him."[22]

Unaware of Willard's skill in such activities, the group made way for the young missionary. His jump easily beat theirs. Cognizant of their surprise, he took off his preacher's coat and hat and handed them to his companion. He proceeded to jump again beating their head mark by two feet. This seemed to startle as well as please them, so he continued by turning a headspring that made a distance of about ten feet.

The preacher-athlete was now an attraction. He continued the side show by turning headsprings, handsprings with one hand and both hands, turning fish-flops, nip-ups, and finally a back somersault. His visually stunning performance thrilled the crowd, and the familiar shrill voice again rang out saying, "Yes, I'd like to see you mob him. He can lick a dozen of you."[23]

While all this activity was going on, Willard was aware of one very interested man standing nearby twisting one side of his mustache as he watched Willard's performance. When the gymnastics demonstration drew to a close, the man approached him, slapped him on the shoulder and said, "You men are going home with me."[24] The grateful missionaries offered no objections.

Their new friend was John Watson, a big-hearted Southerner. He and his wife and two daughters lived less than a half mile up the creek, and he owned 160 acres of the best farm land on the water. Mr. Watson informed them of the original plan of the men in the grove. When they saw Mormon ministers coming, the group

22. Ibid.
23. Ibid.
24. Ibid.

had hurriedly plotted to take them a short distance away, lay them across a fallen tree and lash them with hickory withes.

The Watson family extended their southern hospitality and invited the elders to be their guests for the night. During the evening, Mr. Watson inquired if the pair had seen the white schoolhouse as they left the grove. Acknowledging that they had, he continued, "You are going to preach there next Sunday. That stands on my land, and it is open to all denominations. You are a denomination, and next Sunday is an open date. The other Sabbath days are taken."[25]

Willard informed their friend of their experience with the men at the store near the river and their promise to steer clear of Mine Lick. Mr. Watson assured them that they would be there in force on Sunday—and in good humor. That promise was realized.

John Watson and his entire family were baptized. His oldest daughter married one of the Tennessee missionaries and returned to Utah to live. Their neighbor, Jim Fisher, and four families on the ridge were also baptized.

A New Calling

Upon arrival in Boma the next morning, Willard received a letter from President J. Golden Kimball appointing him president of the Middle Tennessee Conference (or district). This sudden jolt knocked the young missionary groggy.

"Why should this unsought responsibility be saddled on me?" Willard thought. "I was the youngest elder in the conference and, from my standpoint, the least experienced and qualified; and I feared lest the other elders would not take kindly to the appointment. I got a little consolation when I recalled the words of Paul: 'You see your calling, brethren, that not many wise men after the

---

25. Ibid., p. 33.

flesh, not many mighty are called, but God hath chosen the weak things' to accomplish His purposes in the earth."[26]

Willard wrote to the other elders introducing himself with apologies and asking for all their faith and prayers that he might not be a disappointment. In all humility, he feared President Kimball had made a mistake.

Willard and his companion decided to establish headquarters at Smithville, DeKalb County, and set out for their destination pedestrian-style each carrying a heavy valise and small handbag.

With their impending meeting in Mine Lick booked for Sunday, they had just enough time to get to Smithville, park their baggage and arrange for sleeping quarters. A widow woman in town had turned her large home into a small hotel and often offered travelers a place to stay.

Willard explained to the kindly lady who and what they were, declaring that they were non-salaried preachers without remuneration, taking up no collections, and that their labor was a labor of love not a vocation based on salary. She offered to keep them free of charge but said that she would have to ask for a small amount to break even. She retired to another room to discuss the situation with her daughter.

Upon returning, the woman asked the elders if they were willing to sleep two in a bed. They assured her they would sleep three in a bed if necessary. She then said, "I believe we can keep you for 20 cents for each bed and 10 cents for each meal."[27] That seemed too cheap to Willard who told her they would gladly pay 30 cents per bed and 15 cents per meal if she found it necessary to meet expenses.

The apprehensive pair prepared for their Sunday sermon and arrived at John Watson's home Saturday evening. They were informed that there would be a large crowd in attendance Sunday

26. Ibid.
27. Ibid., p. 34.

morning, some coming from the Ridge, Falling Water and Buffalo Valley. The Ridge boys had made plans to take care of the Anderson brothers at the mouth of Mine Lick if trouble arose. The boys from the Ridge were ordinarily peaceful; but when necessary, they were more than anxious to thwart the plans of the Andersons.

Long before meeting time the next morning, people began to trickle in from different directions, some in wagons, others on mules or horseback, but most of them on foot. It was a rather motley assembly being made up mostly of poor people of the tenant farmer class, but all were friendly and hospitable.

Their sermons met with a hearty response, and the congregation requested that they hold an "early candlelight meeting" as there were no provisions made for lighting the building except with lanterns which were scarce in the community. They also requested that another meeting be held a month from that time which was the next open Sunday. The elders readily consented. One man arose after the benediction and said, "I'd like to hear more of this gospel."[28] Others echoed a similar response.

Hidden Talents Surface

Willard was attracted by band music one evening and wandered into the village hall in Smithville to enjoy the performance. Upon inquiry, the band leader learned that Willard was an expert on the snare drum and had played in a band at home. Willard consented when asked to give them pointers and play with the band at the county fair realizing that these little things sometimes made friends for the missionaries.

Every time the elders went to the village for their mail, they passed a beautiful green which was used for a baseball park. Some of the team members were late to practice one day, and the boys needed someone to bat flies for them. Willard volunteered. It came as a great surprise to the boys to see a preacher with such

---

28. Ibid.

athletic ability. He could bat flies and grounders and then catch the ball with equal skill. This, along with his drumming, became common gossip and brought considerable praise from the villagers.

Mission Conference in Mine Lick

Though President Kimball was apprehensive about the location, Willard finalized plans for a mission conference to be held at Mine Lick and assured the president that the people there had become quite friendly towards the Mormons. Willard arranged for sleeping quarters for the president and ten visiting elders and preparations were underway.

The evening before the conference, President Kimball suggested that the elders get together and practice a few songs. Elder Heber C. Iverson, a member of a ward choir in Salt Lake City, was installed as chorister. The first hymn he selected was "Praise to the Man Who Communed with the Heavens." That particular hymn ran quite high in spots, and Willard had to throw his voice into high gear to reach the notes.

They hadn't gotten through the first verse when President Kimball called a halt. "Hold on, brethren," he began. Looking over his glasses, he continued, "Elder Bean, I guess we will have to put you in the other room, bore some holes in the door, and let it in a little at a time. My eardrums won't stand it."[29] Willard obediently toned it down.

At the conference the next morning, it was different. The new converts were used to singing at revival meetings in slow motion and in low gear. They would come in at the end of each line in a demi-semi-quiver about a half line behind the rest of the group. President Kimball couldn't stand it. Leaning over to Willard, he said, "Open her up, Elder Bean. Give 'em both barrels!"[30]

---

29. Ibid., p. 40.
30. Ibid.

The boys from the Ridge were on hand at the conference in case the Anderson boys decided to cause trouble. Rumors were flying about what the Andersons planned for that "damn Mormon Bean,"[31] so every precaution was being taken. Only one of the boys showed his face—and he was so drunk on homemade moonshine that he was easily relieved of his gun and escorted to the creek. There was no further trouble.

A Confrontation

When Willard and his companion returned to Smithville, they found that court was in session. This was a great event in Tennessee and swelled the population of that small town by hundreds with the influx of jurors, witnesses and loiterers.

The two missionaries entered a store on town square to do their shopping and were aware of two or three other men in the store as well. One of them was dressed in ministerial garb and eyed their every move. When the elders started for the door, the insolent minister stepped boldly in front of them. With a high falsetto voice, he began to attract the attention of the loiterers lounging in the shade of nearby trees. Soon a multitude of curious onlookers gathered. The minister started a tirade of abuse, quoting some isolated passages of scripture—or rather misquoting it. Willard correctly quoted the same scriptures adding additional passages which greatly upset the vociferous attacker. As he resorted to abuse, Willard pointed out his beautiful Christian spirit to the body of spectators. The minister became enraged and fairly screamed in an agonized tone of voice.

One of his healers shouted, "I motion we organize a committee and take these men into the woods and attend to their case." An angular-built man past middle age hurried onto the platform and shouted, "You organize a committee to take these men into the

---

31. Ibid.

woods, and there will be another committee organized damned quick. Your man is licked, that's all that makes you squeal."[32]

As if on cue, the minister slunk down in a swoon and two men carried him back to the store and stretched him out on the counter. The man was dead within four days.

Though many in Smithville had become their friends, there were still a great number who felt antagonistic toward the Mormons. On one occasion, the elders were refused lodging 17 times in one evening. When one family finally consented to let them spend the night, they found a note on their doorstep the next morning which read: "To people who keep MORMONS—You'll get a withe in your flank if you allow these raskels to stay here any more. We mean just so. If they are caught here again, all of you will smoke. Truly, Capt. White Caps."[33]

With the usual pistol at the bottom of the note marked "BULL DOG," everyone knew they meant business.

The Debate

The missionaries in Van Buren County had been challenged by a Campbellite minister to debate the plan of salvation. The Campbellites were persistent, and the college students in that town were especially anxious to have the opposing forces meet.

Willard wrote the details to President Kimball asking for his advice on the matter. "Debate him and may the Lord be with you,"[34] was the president's reply. The elders in the district overwhelmingly agreed that Willard was the man for the debate. Feeling less than adequate, he reluctantly consented.

When Willard arrived in Spencer at the appointed time, he found that the whole town had the jitters. The impending debate was the subject of discussion wherever two or more people con-

---

32. Ibid. p. 41.
33. Ibid., p. 43.
34. Ibid., p. 42.

gregated. Willard began to sense the great responsibility resting upon him and passed his concern on to the Lord.

What Willard hoped would be a good night's sleep turned out to be full of agitation—people calling to ask questions; others informing him that his opponent, Reverend Gillentine, had been a pastor for 19 years and was irrefutably qualified to present their doctrines. Gillentine had engaged in numerous debates with Baptists, Presbyterians and Methodists in the past and had an almost flawless record. The articles of agreement for the debate were drawn up as follows: "Resolved that Mormonism, so called, is not the gospel of Jesus Christ according to King James translation of the scriptures."[35]

Each debater was to have four hours and twenty minutes for presentation of his case, rebuttal and summary. Each side selected a moderator. Mr. Baldwin, a Methodist, was chosen to be referee.

Because of his youth and inexperience, Willard was naturally the underdog. Now, as never before, he was impressed by the words of Paul to the Corinthians:

> "For ye see your calling, brethren, how that not many wise men after the flesh, not many mighty, not many noble, are called: but God hath chosen the foolish things of the world to confound the wise; and God hath chosen the weak things of the world to confound the things which are mighty; and base things of the world, and things which are despised, hath God chosen, yea, and things which are not, to bring to nought things that are: that no flesh shall glory in His presence."[36]

The next morning people began to flock in from the country until the chapel was filled to capacity. Many were unable to get inside, so the chapel windows were opened for the benefit of spectators sitting on surrounding lawns to listen to the service.

35. Ibid., p. 50.
36. Ibid. (Also 1 Corinthians 1:26-29)

A ZEALOUS MISSIONARY

After devotional exercises, Reverend Gillentine entered the pulpit arena and opened up a bombardment which lasted a solid hour. He laid his foundation as follows:

"Repent ye and believe the gospel." (He placed repentance before faith.) "If thou believest with all thine heart, thou mayest be baptized." (He failed to place confession before baptism.) The convert is then ready to receive the Spirit— "My word is Spirit." (He said the New Testament is the word of God, hence His Spirit.)[37] This was the sum total of his Plan of Salvation.

During Willard's rebuttal, he quoted scripture that had been previously misquoted as well as much relevant scripture which had not been quoted at all. He also placed quotations in their proper order giving some of them a different interpretation.

At the afternoon session, Willard was first up to bat. He took his text from John 17:3: "And this is life eternal, that they might know thee, the only true God, and Jesus Christ whom thou hast sent."[38]

After quoting ample scripture to prove that the Holy Trinity consisted of three separate personages, he began to weave into the Plan of Salvation. Reverend Gillentine was at a loss to tear down his platform from a Biblical standpoint, so he delved into his satchel and brought out three fiction anti-Mormon books to bolster his argument, adding a little semi-repartee of his own about "Joe Smith" as he called him. His principal stock in trade slanted toward vilification and abuse.

The following morning, Willard gave the opening talk. He first drew the attention of the congregation to the fact that the articles of agreement said they must take King James translation of the scriptures as their sole guide. Reverend Gillentine's repeated slander of the prophet Joseph Smith didn't even please <u>his</u> friends.

---

37. Ibid.
38. Ibid., p. 51.

THE FIGHTING PARSON

Willard asked the congregation how they would feel if he referred to Abraham, Isaac and Jacob as Abe, Ike and Jake; or Peter, James and John as Pete, Jim and Jack. He explained that for 4000 years God had revealed his will to inspired prophets, seers, patriarchs and revelators and that Christ built His church on revelation. He quoted much scripture bearing on that subject.

During the reverend's rebuttal, he again misquoted much scripture—often by design, not by accident. Willard brought to the attention of the congregation that in practically every chapter of the Bible there are words and sometimes entire sentences printed in italics which are not a part of the original scriptures but were added by uninspired translators as they understood them. He pointed out several scriptures whose meanings were drastically changed when the italicized words were omitted.

When Reverend Gillentine stood to deliver his summary, he had little to say. He had shot his last cartridge, so he resorted to his pet hobby of ridicule and vituperation which got him nowhere. Willard had held strictly to the Bible; the overconfident reverend had not.

The Mormon elders received dozens of requests to call on people and stay overnight as a result of the debate. They attended the Methodist Church the next morning and preached the evening sermon by request that night. The professor at the local college invited the missionaries to school the next day and dismissed some of the class periods to give them time to speak to the students.

The youth were especially enthusiastic. "You beat Gillentine at his own game, and we are proud of you. He wasn't even respectful. He got mean and lost his head," was the reaction of one student. Another young observer said, "He had no trouble with beating the Presbyterians and Methodists, but Mormonism is like a porcupine full of quills. You quoted so much scripture that he couldn't penetrate it without pricking his fingers."[39]

---

39. Ibid., p. 52.

Willard passed the credit along to the Lord who is able to mag-
nify "even weak things" to accomplish His purposes.

The "Exhorter Meeting"

An Exhorter Meeting was scheduled to be held in Walker's
Chapel where Willard had made his maiden effort as a missionary.
He couldn't resist the urge to stay overnight and attend the meet-
ing the next evening.

At Exhorter Meetings, novices who felt themselves called to
preach, presided and sermonized. This provided the only opportunity for lay members to display their oratory.

All who had lanterns were asked to bring them to provide the
only light that would be available in the chapel. Willard and his
companion sat in the rear seat of the church which would have
been totally dark except for the lantern provided by their friend
and fellow Mormon, Isaac Bozarth.

After singing a number of revival hymns in slow meter, an exhorter well-known in the community, began to orate. "This good
book," he said as he raised the Bible, "says that Judist was a be-
trater. He at first a good man, but when he betrayed Jesus for a
handful of silver, he turned into a devil and went out and hunged
hisself. I tell you, sinner friends, that Judist was a devil from the
beginnin' and went out and jumped off a cliff and then he was
dead. He was a anti-Christ, a devil, a thief and all them things. He
was chose to be a apostle to do jist what he did done.

"Yes, my sinner friends, we've got Judists right here in DeKalb
County travelin' around from door to door peddlin' their damna-
ble doctrines. And they've baptized some of our women, and they
take them away to Utah and make slaves of 'em. Do you know
where Utah is? Well, I'll tell you. Utah is right in Salt Lake City,
that's where it is. And it's got a big high wall around it, and there's
never been a woman known to get out till they die," etc., etc.[40]

---

40. Ibid., p. 53.

At the close of his somewhat entertaining though offensive tirade, Willard arose from his dismal corner, walked to the front of the chapel, and handed the would-be preacher a couple of tracts asking if he was capable of reading. He answered that he was. Always the missionary, Willard earnestly plead with the preacher to read them prayerfully, digest them, then re-read them. He graciously offered to furnish him with more food for thought when he was ready to receive it.

Campbellite Minister Exposes Mormonism

The Campbellite minister at Walters Hill announced at his Sunday service that he would expose Mormonism the following Sunday. He posted notices to that effect in conspicuous places during the week. Probably thinking his craft was in danger and having been told that all the Mormons had gone back upstate, the minister prepared for the attack.

Willard and his companion, however, had not as yet left town. Knowing the minister's message would be most "inspiring," the elders attended his meeting. When the minister spied them in the congregation, he seemed somewhat confused; but, since he had no other talk prepared, he had little choice but to open up his filthy batteries against the Mormons.

> "When I heard that some Mormon preachers had invaded our community, I felt it my responsibility to check its spread," he began. "So I am here today to expose the greatest and filthiest delusion ever palmed off on to the American public. I warn you, my Christian friends, against being led astray by this damnable heresy now being introduced in our community. If you allow yourselves to be deceived by this delusion, you are on the way to hell there to be ruled over by Satan," etc., etc.[41]

---

41. Ibid., p. 57.

A ZEALOUS MISSIONARY

Even before he had completed his talk, several in the audience approached Willard insisting that he preach at a 2:00 service in the afternoon. He agreed and a prominent citizen made the announcement. The minister was invited to be present. He made several excuses but was prevailed upon by his congregation to accept. They insisted that Willard had listened attentively and respectfully as he spoke, and he owed the same courtesy to the Mormon preacher.

When the afternoon session was about to begin, Willard invited the minister to sit on the rostrum. He refused. Willard then insisted that he at least sit on the front row to give him inspiration. The preacher unwillingly consented.

"I give our brother who spoke from this rostrum today credit for being sincere," Willard began. "I do not hate him for what he said, but rather do I feel sorry for him. He probably thought that he was doing God's service.

"He quoted copiously from Beedle's green-backed fiction novel, probably thinking that this man Beedle was inspired. The same publishing company sent this same man to France to write up the seamy side of life in Paris. This same man was sent to China Town in San Francisco to write up the slimy history of that part of California. He also stopped off in Utah and got some unsavory gossip there. Had he lived in the days of Jesus of Nazareth, he probably would have been with the rabble shouting, 'Crucify him! Crucify him!'

"Surely our brother here would have refrained from accusing Jesus of being a 'blasphemer and guilty of death; a gluttonous man, a friend of Publicans and sinners; a desecrater of the Sabbath; a stirrer up of sedition; a mad man; a man that hath a devil,' or as one writer said, 'They accused him of many things.'

"Jesus said, 'Which of the prophets did not your fathers stone before me?' Deceivers and false prophets may come and go without molestation. It is only God's prophets that are despised and persecuted. It is more blessed to be persecuted than to persecute. 'Blessed are ye when men revile you, and persecute you, and say all manner of evil against you falsely for my sake. Rejoice and be exceeding glad for great is your reward in heaven: for so persecuted they the prophets which were before you....Blessed are you when men shall hate you, and when they shall separate you from their company, and shall reproach you, and cast your name as evil, for the Son of Man's sake....Woe unto you when all men speak well of you for so did their fathers to the false prophets....Be ye therefore merciful, as your Father is merciful. Judge not that ye be not judged. Condemn not and ye shall not be condemned. Forgive and ye shall be forgiven.'

"Yes, brother, persecution is an heritage of God's people," Willard continued. "All who live godly in Christ Jesus shall suffer persecution. Sinful, wicked people are not persecuted for righteousness sake. . . .The Devil was a liar from the beginning because he is a liar and the father of it. Persecution is Satan's chief weapon, but he does not persecute men who preach false doctrine. He does inspire them to carry on their nefarious work. Now, brother, in which of these categories do you function? Believing that you know not what you do, I whole-heartedly forgive."[42]

Willard continued his sermon on the subjects of charity and repentance. At its conclusion, the guest minister arose and beckoned for the congregation to remain seated. He had been weeping, which Willard observed, and his eyes were still wet. He made a confession that he had probably been led astray by prejudiced literature. He humbly apologized, then explained, "While I was yet a boy, I heard my parents read a book accusing the Mormon people of many things. I believed what they read. Later I read other

42. Ibid., p. 58.

books and articles about Mormons, and I have been led to believe they were a licentious people. I now believe that I was mistaken. I supposed, until now, that they did not believe in our Bible but had supplanted our Bible and that they have a Bible of their own. Elder Bean, I now promise you and this congregation that I shall never vilify or misrepresent the Mormon people again."[43]

He stepped forward and shook Willard's hand warmly.

The Mormon Massacre

Willard served 26 months as a missionary in the Southern States Mission. He was less than overjoyed when he received a letter from his new mission president, Elias Kimball, announcing his release. He felt he was just getting to the point where he could do more efficient and effective missionary work. With a bit of sadness in his soul, he wrote to each pair of elders under his jurisdiction, as well as the saints and other friends in his mission, bidding them goodbye. He left Nashville, Tennessee, on April 4, 1895.

With his release came another assignment. Willard was asked to visit some saints in Lewis County and visit the Condor farm on Cane Creek where a massacre had taken place a few years before. His assignments included getting a photograph of the house and interviewing the people in the area if he determined it safe to do so. He was also to call on Finley Hauser near Lawrenceburgh to get definite information concerning the massacre.

Finley was delighted to see Willard as there hadn't been a Mormon in the territory for several years. Finley directed him to the home of John Anthony who had lived on Cane Creek near the Condor farm when the incident occurred. Describing the melee, Mr. Anthony said:

"The Mormon elders were preparing to hold a meeting at the Condor farm. A mob was organized, rubbed charcoal on their faces, some wore White-Cap uniforms. They went

43. Ibid.

to the Condor farm to stop the meeting—if needs be by force. More than half of them took guns with them just in case the Condor boys put up a fight. Nearly one hundred agreed to gather at 9:00 A.M., but not more than half of them showed up. They were singing some hymns when the mobbers came in sight.

"There was considerable commotion and one of the Condor boys grabbed a gun from over the door intending to protect the elders; but Doc Plummer, who seemed to be one of the leaders of the mobocrats, grabbed the gun and while struggling for possession of it another member of the mob shot the Condor boy killing him instantly. At this point one of the Mormon elders went out the back door and made his escape into the woods.

"Now shooting became general," Mr. Anthony went on. "One of the elders fell mortally wounded. The other Condor boy got hold of a gun; but before he got to use it, he was shot dead. Another Mormon elder was seen to slump to the floor and died without a struggle. Mrs. Condor was badly wounded and was thrown onto a bed. There were three Hinson boys in the mob, and it is said that one of the Condor boys shot and killed Babe Hinson, the leader of the mobbers, before he himself was killed. There were more than 20 shots fired during the melee. Most of the mobbers, if not all, had been drinking. The leader of the mob was shot in the front yard, and after the shooting ceased they began to hurry away. A brother of the badly-wounded Hinson boy shouted for them to help carry his brother or they would get some of the same medicine. Some returned, but they only carried the boy about 100 yards when he begged them to stop. They placed him down on the hillside and he died in a few minutes."[44]

---

44. Ibid., p. 75.

A ZEALOUS MISSIONARY

After hearing the bloody details from Brother Anthony, Willard decided it was time to head for Lewis County where the incident actually took place. He retired his clergy garb and donned his new roust-about suit which was purchased especially for this occasion. Wanting to avoid any similarity to a preacher and especially any resemblance to a Mormon, Willard decided to play the part of a timber inspector. His family in Sevier County, Utah, had worn out a mill or two, and he was expert at all mill jobs from piling lumber to sawyer to rafting logs down the river.

Willard was directed to a small hotel in the town of Mannie where transient mill workers gathered to swap stories and peddle local gossip. Willard casually broke into the conversation and eventually inquired about the "incident that gave their county some publicity a few years ago."[45]

One of the ladies present said, "I guess Tom here knows as much about that affair as anybody in the village. But I know one thing—there's been no Mormons here since."[46]

Tom, a man past middle life, offered, "No, the Mormons don't trouble us no more. They had some trouble over on the creek and I reckon got fixed good and plenty. They'd been warned to get out of the county mor'n once, but they jest kep on preachin'. I reckon they soon learnt that the people in these parts mean what they say. They bragged that if the White Caps got any of 'em, God would raise up four for every one they got. But our boys got four of 'em and God haint sent none yet. And what they wus left in these parts got out damn quick and none haint showed up since."[47]

Tom continued his macabre report. "The Mormons fit back all right, but might-a-knowd they wus up agin it. Yes, they shot one of the Hinson boys and when they did they got a damned good

45. Ibid., p. 76.
46. Ibid.
47. Ibid.

man. No, there haint no Mormons here now, and I reckon they'll never bother us again."[48]

Another gentleman in the tavern offered additional information. "I went down next morning along with some more men and looked the old house over," he said. "It was a sorry sight all right. Puddles of blood all over the floor and a puddle or two in the yard. The old lady got shot in the hip, but I reckon it was accidental-like. But when we wus there she was layin' on the bed sufferin' and moanin' to beat hell. She didn't die though, and I hear'n she moved to Perry County."[49]

When Willard inquired as to the present sentiment relative to Mormons, one lady spoke up. "The sentiment is that we'ns don't want no more Mormons in these parts. One of the Hinson boys was hear'n to say, 'If the Mormons turned up again, they'd wind up in a graveyard.'"[50]

Not wishing to agitate matters further and detract their attention from their games, Willard changed the subject.

The next morning, the incognito elder again found opportunity to engage in casual conversation with a few of the townsfolk. Everyone's interpretation of the incident was pretty much the same with the addition of the appearance of a Mormon preacher down by the spring a short distance from the Condor house. The mob left one man to guard him with instructions to shoot the preacher and hurry to the house if shooting started. The preacher turned pale and began to plead for his life. He looked pitiful and begged so earnestly that the guard told him to hurry and get out of sight when the shooting began. The guard then pointed his rifle toward the sky and shot it before hastening to the house.

One man in the group was conspicuous by his silence. When he found himself alone with Willard, he offered new insight. Most of the bad publicity the Mormons had received was due to a news-

48. Ibid., p. 77.
49. Ibid.
50. Ibid.

paper article which had been published in Lawrenceburgh, he revealed.

"Among other things," the man confided, "the article stated that when a woman was led into the water for baptism that the elder leaned over and whispered to her saying, 'Now after you are baptized and sanctified you are a sister of the church and become as much my wife as you are your husband's and whatsoever thou doest thou sinnest not.' Certain prejudiced men took that newspaper all through the county for people to read and those who couldn't read had it read to them. The ignorant class accepted it as gospel truth. The few of us who didn't believe it played safe by not expressing our views."[51]

The Mysterious Robert Edge

After gathering all possible information on the Condor farm incident and the death of the two elders (Elder Biggs and Elder Berry), Willard boarded a train and proceeded to Lexington to investigate the "mysterious preacher," Robert Edge. After interviewing several businessmen and others, he walked seven miles to Perryville where Edge did most of his preaching. This is what he learned:

A man named Robert Edge, about 45 years of age, about 5 feet 9 or 10 inches in height, kept himself well-dressed but not in clerical garb. He came from nowhere and disappeared just as mysteriously. He was an eloquent man, a good scriptorian, teaching doctrines more than ethics. He told them to bring their Bibles to church and mark the quotations he used.

After preaching on the necessity and mode of baptism, several persons applied to be baptized. He quoted scripture saying, "Paul may sow, Appolus water, but God giveth the increase." He refused to baptize them saying that ere long men would come who would baptize them and would preach the same doctrines he had taught.

---

51. Ibid., p. 80.

Some time later Mormon elders came into their midst and baptized a goodly number. Later these converts moved to Colorado and settled in San Louis Valley and Manassa.

This preacher took up no collections but did accept small gratuities to cover expenses. Nobody seemed to know what became of him. The only clue they gave was that they had heard of a similar preacher in North Carolina.[52]

Willard Returns Home

Like the majority of missionaries, Willard returned home richer in experience but financially embarrassed. His early schooling had been greatly neglected having been shortened on both ends—in the fall to clear the fields of livestock and in the spring to work at the sawmill.

Willard returned to Provo, Utah, to find that track athletics and football were just being introduced at the Brigham Young Academy. This provided just the right enticement to register for college.

"I don't know how I got in as I was not asked to take any examination, but probably admitted on general principles,"[53] he said.

---

52. Ibid., p. 82.
53. Ibid., p. 83.

BORN OF GOODLY PARENTS

W hat kind of environment produces a man like Willard Bean? What kind of example did he follow in his formative years?

Willard's father, George Washington Bean, was a picture of strength and dedication. His very name was symbolic of the patriotism and love of country and family that made this land great. He was one of the valiant Mormon pioneers in 1847 who ably led many companies of saints to the great Salt Lake Valley.

George admitted that when he was a youngster, he "endured the jibes of 'Pa's shadow' to glean information on the business of farming and cattle raising"[1] as his father counseled with his hired hands. He was always anxious to learn and confided he was "all ears and eyes, and always have been when there is anything to learn."[2]

His mother, Elizabeth Lewis Bean, was instrumental in forming George's personality and teaching peace in the home. She "kept bad words washed from our tongues, and ended children's quarrels by finding jobs far apart,"[3] he recorded in his journal.

George's parents were strictly religious—his father being a Methodist and his mother a Presbyterian. Mormonism was first introduced in their home town of Mendon, Illinois, in 1840 when Alexander Williams, one of the Mormon exiles from Missouri, be-

1. George Washington Bean Autobiography and Family Record, by Flora Bean Horne, copyright 1945, p. 15, in possession of Vicki Bean Topliff, Orem, Utah (hereafter cited as G. W. Bean, Autobiography).
2. Ibid.
3. Ibid., p. 16.

came possessed with a desire to learn reading, writing and grammar at the Bean's local school. Many of the saints driven from Missouri sought refuge in that area of Adams County.

Alexander was older than the other students, but was earnest and devoted to his lessons. He was blessed with a great deal of personal magnetism as well as with the spirit of the gospel, and he and George became fast friends.

Alexander was invited to the Bean home and religious discussions were inevitable. George's mother, herself a scriptorian, soon became very much surprised at the clearness of the Mormon's views and explanations of the scriptures. The Beans began to understand the Bible in an entirely new light.

As a result, Alexander baptized James and Elizabeth Bean in May of 1841. George's sister, Nancy, and several neighbors and their families were baptized as well. George followed suit on July 12, 1841.

By the time George was ten years old, he had developed quite a reputation for having a good memory and learning his lessons well at school. It was not uncommon for him to go up to five miles away to spell down an entire school. "I found by studying the root words that I could spell and define any words coming from that original word,"[4] he said.

The Family Settles in Nauvoo

The Bean family soon moved to Nauvoo and built a brick house two blocks south of the temple site. At the age of 14, George was put to work on the temple in an effort to speed up the work and avoid the enemies of the church who were determined to hinder its progress. George spent most of his time that summer on the roof and tower handling timbers.

---

4.   Ibid., p. 19.

Mobbings and burnings took place in Nauvoo in September of 1845. Hundreds of houses were burned, stock was driven off and crops were destroyed. Captain Stephen A. Markham mustered a posse of 120 men forming the Nauvoo Legion. George was one of that number. The men rode on horseback night and day with arms and full equipment for any emergency. They soon scattered the "wicked hosts of Satan"—some fleeing into the state of Missouri before feeling safe.

George considered his stint with the Nauvoo Legion to be his first real public service. At 14 he was large in stature and well built and did his full share of duty for five days and nights. He continued to perform night guard duty all winter on the streets of Nauvoo.

Just two months later, in November 1845, George was ordained a Seventy by Joseph Young (Brigham's son). He received his own endowments in the Nauvoo Temple before he was 15 years of age.

The Exodus to Salt Lake

Persecution became more severe in Nauvoo. George and other members of the church prepared to flee their Illinois home. George recorded their departure this way:

"As the twenty thousand Latter-day Saints prepared to leave the State of Illinois, the shops and homes and Temple and foods were guarded. The Mississippi river was open to ferryboats early in February, 1846, so we helped the officials to safety into Iowa. About the 20th, Father had me fitted up to proceed with the Camp of Israel in starting for the wilderness. After ferrying the Church leaders, their families and effects across that great river, we younger fry joined the ranks."[5]

Traveling conditions were far from ideal. Much suffering prevailed. A great deal of grumbling and, in some cases, almost open rebellion resulted. Many slept on the ground and got soaking wet almost every night. Rations and supplies became short. Roads

5. Ibid., p. 24.

were virtually impassable for some time and much insubordina-
tion manifested itself.

"Sometimes we were reduced to only bread made of parched
corn meal, which, when somewhat old is about as nourishing as
so much sawdust or bran, and some of us got pretty lean,"[6] George
commented in his journal.

The only comfort the saints felt in leaving their newly-built
homes in Nauvoo, their farms and their cattle, was that "Joseph
our Prophet saw in a vision our homes in the Mountains a year or
so before he was martyred. He knew another Prophet would be
raised up to lead us there. We had faith that his prophecy would
come true, and we faced the West unafraid."[7]

The Bean temper, which was slow to kindle but was known to
erupt in George as well as in future generations, was manifest one
day during the long trek to Salt Lake.

That flare-up almost caused the court martial of that 16-year-
old lad. George was accused of "assault and battery on the person
of Gabe Mayberry."[8]

George gave this account:

"The night before my combat with Gabe, our captain decided to correct the slowness of certain ones who kept the
rest of us waiting so often, by saying that the first one in
line the next morning could lead our company. This sixteen
year old boy was up and ready and in place in head of lazy
Gabe. My conscience was clear as I won my place, but it
angered him and he began to reek vengeance upon my
oxen. I leaped to the rescue of my faithful friends, and fairly
shouted: 'You can beat me if you like, but not my oxen.' He
lashed away at them again and I cracked him over the head

---

6. Ibid., p. 26-27.
7. Ibid., p. 27-28.
8. Ibid., p. 35.

with the butt of my ox whip....I worried for days about the court-martial, but my prayers were answered."[9]

The outcome looked bleak for George at the proceedings until Jedediah M. Grant (Second Counselor to President Brigham Young and father of Heber J. Grant) asked permission to say a few words. He pointed out that a man's teams were his salvation on such a journey. He felt to "honor the lad who would fight in defense of his team if need be, and that a man should be punished for laziness, if possible, instead of putting a premium on it."[10]

John Young also came to George's aid. Largely due to the testimonies of these two men, judgment was not rendered and George walked forth a free lad.

"When Brother Grant began to talk, my spirit began to revive and by the time he got through, I felt that I was about a foot higher than just before," George recorded.

"Uncle John Young also spoke in the same strain and oh, how thankful and grateful I did feel. Here was I, a lone boy of sixteen, far away from parents and kindred, brought to trial for an act that was just as natural for a boy of spirit as it was to breathe, and just at the time that all hope was lost, to get relief from the highest authority at that time—well, suffice it to say, that the judgment was not rendered, and I walked forth a free lad, and my good old Capt. Vance never afterwards required me to travel behind Gabe Mayberry. I can truly say from that day forward I never found the person who stood higher in my estimation for good, pure, unalloyed principle and righteous judgment than Pres. Jedediah M. Grant, as also Uncle John Young, and many is the time thereafter that I would fly to aid the old gentleman in yoking his cattle, greasing his wagon, etc."[11]

9. Ibid.
10. Ibid., p. 36.
11. Ibid., p. 36.

George's company struggled on through many other trials and finally reached the Salt Lake Valley on October 4, 1847. Several other companies had already reached the valley. Simply stated but dramatically felt were these words in George's journal: "These were the times that tried men's souls, and women's, too."[12]

The first day of 1848 was properly observed by breaking up and sowing one acre of land with three pecks of wheat. More planting was done in the spring, but living was very scanty for a time. The Bean's cow gave milk and they had a little flour, so they had thickened milk, or "lumpy dick" as they called it, three times a day for several weeks.

Crickets Infest the Land

The great cricket catastrophe that devastated the early Mormon settlers erupted in that settlement in 1848.

"When the crops came up and gave hope of foodstuff and grain, it was not lasting," George wrote, "for hoards of great black crickets came marching down the hillsides, and the way our corn disappeared was a caution. We fought them pretty well for some days by plowing deep furrows all around and filling them with water, but they soon got smart enough to drop in and paddle around and across to the other side. We drove them into brush fires, we flailed them, but they seemed to increase. A 'fast day' of prayer and supplication was held by the Saints."

"When they went to the fields and the sun became darkened, a combination of faith and fear came over them, until the Sea Gulls alighted in the fields, and the way these little birds worked for our Salvation was pleasing to see. They were about the size of tame pigeons and they would come by thousands and gobble up those great fat crickets that were as large as a man's thumb, until they would get about a pint, seemingly, then they would adjourn to the water ditch, take a drink and throw up all their crickets—rest

---

12. Ibid., p. 37.

themselves a little, then back to slaying the black 'monsters' again. They continued this and the crickets were destroyed, and most of some crops. Some planted seeds again."[13]

George Becomes Mediator Between Mormons and Indians

With the cricket melee behind them, the Bean family answered the call for a colony of settlers to locate at Provo early in the spring of 1849. George assisted in building Fort Utah in the center of which was erected a bastion 30 feet square on strong posts 10 or 12 feet high. A six-pounder cannon was mounted on top to guard against Indian troubles.

In President Brigham Young's desire to make friends with all the Indian tribes, he called Orrin Porter Rockwell and George Bean to his office to ask their assistance in carrying a message of "friendship-peace" to the Indians. "We were humble, yet fearless, because the Prophet of the Lord had called us to service. We accepted it,"[14] George said.

The Indians were in their war paint and were holding war dances around their campfires when Porter and George approached their reservation. The two men moved cautiously and prayerfully.

"I never carried a gun on any Indian mission but Porter always was well armed since the days of the mobbings of Nauvoo, and wore his hair long, which my wife often braided for him at night when he stayed at our home."[15] (Joseph Smith told Porter that he would never be killed by the enemy as long as he didn't cut his hair.)

As the two men neared the Indian camp, they agreed, "If we both go on horseback, we'll be killed." After some discussion, Por-

---

13. Ibid., p. 39.
14. Ibid., p. 53.
15. Ibid.

ter said, "George, you go to the Camp alone. You know the language and maybe some of the Indians. Your personality is better than mine, too. I'll hide in these willows, ready to rush to you when you give the signal." George added: "And Brother Brigham sent us with a message of Peace, and a 'God Bless you,'" so he proceeded without fear.[16]

George gave these details of the incident:

"As I neared the camp, I saw them dancing about a bonfire, with their paints and feathers, and squaws beating tomtoms. When they saw a man coming, they feared, and three 'bucks' came out to meet me, tied my hands behind me and took me to their camp (one on each side of me and one walking behind me), and stood me on a buffalo robe and there I stood for two hours. I was not permitted to say a word until after they related all their bad feelings; boasted over their depredations and successful battles with other tribes, too numerous to mention; and told what they expected to do with the 'Whites' now stealing their hunting grounds, and how the crows would pick our bones, etc. Being over six feet tall, much taller than any of them, and stretching up still taller as they talked, calm and fearless, there I stood for two long hours. When they saw I was not afraid but friendly, one war-horse Indian after another slunk away saying: 'OAH, OAH' with appropriate gesture, meaning 'all right.' The 'Gift of Interpretation' was given to me, as I called it, for I understood every word they said, even to each other. The tomtoms tapered down and the Chief said: 'Now you talk.' There I stood on the significant buffalo robe, over six feet of manhood, full of gratitude, my hands were loosed. I delivered the message of friendship from the 'White Chief' Brigham Young, who represented the 'Great Spirit' in his feelings toward the Indians and all mankind, a brotherly feeling that must last forever, etc. The dancers

16. Ibid.

stopped and listened, for they were as tired as I, perhaps, and their rituals were over, and Chiefs Walker, Sow-i-ette and Sub-Chief accompanied me to where Porter Rockwell held our horses. As I had given no signal, he thought I had been killed, and I feared for him, but not myself. Porter also delivered the word from Brigham, the 'White Chief.' They decided we were true messengers, and gave a promise of Peace. We had learned much of Indian ideals and customs and expressions. I could follow all they said but could not answer until permitted. When friendship was agreed, we mounted our horses and rode away. Many of those Indians became friendly and became protectors of my life, and warned the people, through me, of dangers. I was eighteen years old at this time, but grown up through hard experiences."[17]

The Great Cannon Explosion

On September 1, 1849, as George and his father returned from work, Lieutenant William Dayton called to George to help him test fire the cannon at Fort Utah. The lad quickly responded and hurried up the ladder to the platform that housed the cannon. They fired once, and then, without swabbing the gun, Lt. Dayton "caught up another cartridge of old cotton cloth and 1½ pounds of rifle powder, inserted it in the muzzle and we both began ramming the cartridge home, when it evidently caught fire, being broken and torn, and the remnant of the former one still burning in the breech, caused a disastrous explosion. It caused a deafening roar"[18] which sent into shock all within hearing distance. The two men were thrown thirty feet away on the ground, and Lt. Dayton was killed outright. George was dying, his body terribly mangled; but he was still breathing. His left hand was gone—"picked up in Celia Hunt's dooryard, who recognized George Bean's band ring

---

17. Ibid., p. 53-54.
18. Ibid., p. 57.

on his little finger."[19] His clothes were partly burned off, his eyes and face were black with powder and burned so badly he lost his sight. His right arm and hand were severely lacerated. His right thigh, breast, neck and face were filled with splinters and powder burn. Some of the two hundred splinters remained in his body working their way to the surface at different times during the next twenty years of his life.

Immediately following the explosion, George's mangled body was carried to his home where it remained for forty days. As he regained consciousness, hopes of saving his life heightened.

"My parents and friends sat during the night watching my every breath as if it might be my last, yet praying for me and the Doctor's arrival," he recorded.

"They were relieved when daylight came and Dr. Blake walked in. Of course I had to rely on Father's report on which was done first. Dr. Blake removed his cloak, donned his medical gown, made hasty examinations of my black powder burned face and neck, and then ordered all out of the room except his aids and Father. He then proceeded to saw the bones of my left forearm, leaving a three-and-a-half-inch stub below the elbow, which served me well all my life. Of course in those days people had to endure pain in operations by the will power of the injured, as mothers bore their children without an anesthetic. Dr. Blake was an expert. He had to probe into my flesh for those 200 hickory ramrod slivers, some of which seemed to go to the bones. The largest was taken from my right thigh, being three inches long and the size of a lead pencil. How I ever stood all that probing is a marvel to me yet, but all my friends were praying for me, and miracles do happen at times, as the Lord designs.

---

19. Ibid., p. 58.

"Each day for a week or ten days, Dr. Blake dressed my wounds and probed for more splinters—first from neck, chest and abdomen where hard wood slivers might enter vital organs, until he had 200 splinters in my mother's fruit jar. My heart tonic was sweetened hot water with brandy in it. Beef tea was my nourishment because I could not chew, and wondered if I ever could. With my eyes scabbed over like my whole face, I wondered if I could ever see again. My patient mother did everything to ease my pain and give comfort, although she, too, was wondering. Faithful friends came in to join Father in administrations, but I could not see them. The days were long and the nights longer, as I suffered in every inch of my body, and prayed so hard to die. The future looked so dark to me.

"About three weeks after the accident, a miracle was performed by three Prophets of the Lord who entered our humble home. They were President Brigham Young, Heber C. Kimball and Willard Richards. Why did these three men, the Presidency of The Church of Jesus Christ in these latter days, come to see and bless an insignificant eighteen year old boy like me?

"They visited with Mother a bit while Father shuffled off his farm clothes to join them. Their presence brought calmness. They evidently saw my condition, but I could not see them, but recognized their voices from hearing them preach. Mother appealed to them—'Brother Brigham, do you think he can live?' 'Of course he can, and will,' he answered. Then he came to me, took my hand, the right hand, the only one I had —and asked: 'George, do you want to live?' His very handshake gave me strength, and I answered: 'Yes, if I can do any good,' with my weak voice, trembling. President Young then said: 'Then you shall live.' He called his counselors to my bed, my Mother brought the consecrated oil, one of them anointed my head and the other sealed that anointing. Then 'Brother Brigham' gave me a marvelous blessing. He rebuked the power of the Destroyer from my body and from our home. It was like an electric current that ran through me from head to foot and it took the severe pain with it. He plead with the Lord to heal me from head to foot that all wounds might heal quickly, and that faith may increase as the healing takes place and that I may ever rejoice in God's blessings in performing the works He has for me to do, etc. How I wish I had that blessing in writing. He made plain to me that the Holy Ghost, bestowed upon me after baptism, would be my constant guide and educator, and that the Lord's work assigned to me will be gloriously completed."[20]

George's parents rejoiced with him as they listened to the words of "Brother Brigham." They were "lifted above all earthly things in rejoicing with the Prophets of the Lord in humility and sincere brotherly love."[21]

The next day, the scales fell from George's eyes, and he saw light for the first time in twenty days.

During his illness, he had many visits from friendly Indians who sympathized with his sufferings. He used this time to learn more of the Indian language, and, in turn, teach them some English. George truly believed that the incident was a blessing in disguise which enabled him to "clinch the Indian Language gift" he had received and proved immeasurably useful in later years as the saints dealt with the Indians.

George and Elizabeth are Wed

On September 29, 1852, the first thrill of love came to young George Bean. It was the custom at that time for those who had crossed the plains to renew their covenants by being rebaptized. As Ward Clerk, George was in attendance when two new arrivals from Council Bluffs, Iowa, came to be rebaptized—Jane and Eliz-

20. Ibid., p. 59-60.
21. Ibid., p. 61.

abeth Baum, "rosy cheeked and attractive, especially the younger one, Elizabeth."[22]

Elizabeth, the daughter of Jacob Baum and Agnes Harris, had been born in Brandywine, Chester County, Pennsylvania, on January 27, 1834. Her father was a prosperous Dutch farmer, a skilled weaver, spinner, fuller, carder, and more, and Elizabeth had been the beneficiary of this artistic training. When her parents heard the gospel message in 1842, they readily accepted it and were baptized. At the age of nine, Elizabeth moved with her family to Nauvoo where they bought a farm six miles from the city. She was baptized in the Mississippi River in May 1845.

Elizabeth remembered until the time of her death her acquaintance as a small girl with the Prophet Joseph Smith. She vividly recalled the day the bodies of the martyred prophet and his brother, Hyrum, were taken past her father's farm en route from Carthage to Nauvoo. At age 12, she witnessed Brigham Young being recognized as the man to be the new leader of the Mormon Church.

Elizabeth and her family were driven from Nauvoo with the other members of the Church. While at Winter Quarters, they plowed considerable land and raised crops for those in need. Her mother died at Council Bluffs in 1846 leaving 12-year-old Elizabeth and her father with the responsibility of the family of younger children.

In 1852, Elizabeth and her family left the Bluffs and headed west. Exceptionally capable for her years, Elizabeth drove two yoke of oxen most of the way. In September they arrived in the Salt Lake Valley. They camped a few miles south of the city for five days and then went on to Provo where they bought a log cabin in the northern part of the village.

It was in this humble setting that George and Elizabeth first met. As the young ward clerk's eyes met those of the sweet new Dutch girl, they both felt an instant warmth and excitement.

---

22. Ibid., p. 86.

It was a short courtship. The Baum girls were using a covered wagon as their room while their adobe house was being enlarged; and it was in that wagon, by the light of a candle and the warmth created by a pan of coals, that Elizabeth made her wedding gown. They were married by Bishop Isaac Higbee on January 6, 1853, and were later sealed in the Endowment House in Salt Lake City.

George Is Almost Sent to the "Happy Hunting Ground"

Just one year after their marriage, George's life was miraculously spared through the intercession of one of his truest Indian friends, "Squash" Washear. George was sitting at the desk in his cabin when the Ute Indian Doctor came in. He was in mourning and related to George the sad story of the death of his squaw and papoose. He was searching for some good person to go with them to the "Happy Hunting Ground," and "then he waxed eloquent in praise of me, as he drew closer. Elizabeth saw the point of the Doctor's knife blade extending below his blanket he had thrown about him, and shouted: 'George, don't you see that knife?' which gave the Doctor his cue to strike his deadly blow."[23]

He raised his knife to strike when Squash, like a flash, threw up his bow and arrows and deflected the blow of the knife, thus saving George's life.

The Doctor returned the next day to ask forgiveness. He said he was so sad over the death of his squaw and child, he was "almost crazy and didn't realize he was going to kill the best friend the Indians had."[24]

This event gave greater cause for renewed missionary work among the Indians. The custom of killing another to accompany the dead to the "Happy Hunting Ground" had been discouraged before, but now they needed to be much more explicit on the displeasure it brings to the "Great Spirit"—to say nothing of the men they considered their "best friends."

23. Ibid., p. 101.
24. Ibid.

George Builds Rapport with the Indians

In that same year, President Brigham Young called on Orrin Porter Rockwell and George Bean again, this time assigning them the task of keeping Chief Walker in hand and peaceable for a year even if it cost the Church $10,000. He asked them to labor, teach and trade among the Utah Indians in an effort to heal up the feelings made by previous occurrences.

George acted as mediator for both sides. Not only did President Young request his services in dealing with the Indians, but the Indians came to George to settle their disputes with the white men. When the Indians were told not to kill deer out of season, they became hostile. They believed the deer belonged to them. The only way the white men could keep them from killing deer was to mark and brand them, they said. The white people were also accused of stealing their fish. They insisted all the fish belonged to them.

George, fortunately, had developed a good rapport with the red men. He and his children let them play lacrosse on their salt-grass flat. They gave them flour and taught them how to make bread and shared their freshly-killed beef and hogs with them. They were well aware that Indians made good friends but bad enemies. (Willard especially enjoyed wrestling and playing games with the young Indian boys. They called him Ka-pu-rats toats which meant "one-armed man's boy.")

A Great Pioneer

George spent the better part of his life being a pioneer. He traveled hundreds of miles on foot or in covered wagons or ox carts assisting companies of saints to the Salt Lake Valley. He was hired to lead exploration parties in search of new and better routes to other states. When the United States Army invaded Utah in 1857, George was sent to Carson Valley to instruct the Mormons to hastily return to Utah. At the prophet's call in 1858, he explored the desert regions west of Fillmore and Beaver in search of hiding places in case Johnston's Army came in.

This able lad was a pioneer in dealing with the Indians and was sent on a mission to Las Vegas, Nevada, to call the "savages" to repentance. On April 22, 1855, George received a special blessing from Apostle Wilford Woodruff setting him apart for his mission among the Lamanites. Among other things he said:

> "Thou shalt be mighty and have influence among the seed of Joseph and thou shalt teach them to leave off all their foolishness, their shedding of blood and all their filthy and evil practices and abominations of every description. There-fore go forth with thy brethren and be full of faith before the Lord and He shall raise thee up and make thee use-ful in imparting the knowledge of the English language to thy brethren the Lamanites and of impressing upon their minds the truths contained in the Book of Mormon and the Prophecies of the ancient prophets who lived upon this Continent and who bore record of the great blessings that should rest upon their descendants, after that their curse and afflictions should be removed and they become a de-lightsome people."[25]

George had ten days to prepare for his departure. "Having some money I bought up a bin full of wheat, some land, but this being the great grasshopper year in Utah there was nothing much raised in the fields. We had several cows, etc., and some cash, leaving the wife and child, my most concern, well provided for, so my thoughts were at ease,"[26] he recorded.

In his journal, he wrote: "We got along fairly well during the winter with teaching these untutored sons of Laman and Lemuel their origin and the Gospel of Christ as well as cleanliness, hon-esty, industry and love of the 'Great Spirit' they seemed to fear, yet recognize. Some were added to our number that winter."[27]

---

25. Ibid., p. 116.
26. Ibid., p. 117.
27. Ibid., p. 123.

Polygamy Becomes a Reality for George

Shortly after returning home from Las Vegas, George received a call from Brigham Young requesting that he adopt the practice of plural marriage. After counseling with his wife Elizabeth, she concluded: "I know the principle as designed by God is correct, if lived righteously; but if you can't do that, stay out of it. If you can, I am agreed."[28]

George, too, had seen men disgrace the principle and themselves, but recalled an eloquent discourse given by Elder Orson Pratt in 1851 in support of the plan. Elder Pratt had enabled his listeners to view the grand platform for eternity. Together, George and Elizabeth decided to accept the responsibility of a polygamous marriage.

Emily Haws became George's second wife on December 10, 1856. He married Mary Jane Wall just a few days later on December 15. Elizabeth agreed with his choice of brides and stood by his side at the ceremonies.

Between the years 1854 and 1884, George became the father of thirty children, three of whom died in infancy. The remaining 27 grew to be intelligent, active citizens—active in both church and community. His advice to his children was: "Never refuse to do service in the Church. It is the best school in the world."[29]

Making One Hand Do for Two

George's children, along with others, marveled at how he learned to make one hand do for two. Using the soap, wash rag and towel were easy, but it took discipline and practice to become proficient in harnessing the mules and putting on the brake and handling four lines going into a hollow as well as releasing the brakes when ascending. He could cut his own fingernails by placing his pocket knife on his left knee and holding it firmly with his

---

28. Ibid., p. 126.
29. Ibid., p. 210.

stub arm, then twisting his right hand about it. He learned to place the harness on his riding animals and saddle his ponies, drive a four-horse team and handle stubborn mules; but the two most difficult things for him were "buttoning that celluloid collar on a shirt and tying the bow."[30] He was grateful when someone invented a hook on the tie to slide over the collar button.

Another problem he faced was cutting his meat at the table. He could eat like the cowboys and Indians around a campfire but couldn't lower himself to such indignities at the dinner table with his family. He set his brain buzzing to find a remedy. The result? A combination knife and fork for one-handed folks—himself especially. The knife part was to cut the food, and the fork to convey it to the mouth. Though he had no desire to patent his invention, the company that made the instrument gave him credit for it in a magazine article.

The Beans Join the United Order

George was an early pioneer in the establishment of the United Order. The small town of Prattville caught the spirit, and members of George's expanding family joined the throng. His daughters, Elizabeth, Melinda and Geneva, taught in the United Order. George and his boys set to work grubbing and clearing ground. Many men and teams from the Order were sent to Grass Valley to give the Indians a start on their farms.

Anti-Polygamy Law Passes

The notorious Edmunds Anti-Polygamy Law passed Congress in 1883. This law disfranchised three or four thousand leading members of the Church but legitimized all children born prior to January 1, 1883. Apostates became active in reporting their neighbors to the government officials getting their "special price" for their services.

---

30. Ibid., p. 125.

"This did not hinder my family unity in spirit, or in planting and harvesting crops, or in public services. My neighbor shouted out one day as children from my three families rode from the field on a load of potatoes—'Hurrah! See the Beans and potatoes.'"[31]

Some leading authorities of the Church were sent to prison because they would not deny and desert their plural wives and their children. Others went into hiding while trying to carry on personal matters and church business as best they could.

In 1887 the Tucker Amendment to the Edmunds Law was passed which confiscated the LDS Church property and took away any legal right they may have had in appealing their cases. The penitentiary was filled with cohabitation cases, along with real criminals.

In an effort to find a way to retain his liberty, George asked permission of the Presiding Bishop, William Preston, to be "emigrated" temporarily to Rexburg, Idaho. Permission was granted. Some time later, on December 16, 1888, George wrote this letter to his family while feeling the pangs of loneliness in his exiled state:

"My dear family, wives and children:

"It is with very peculiar feelings that I attempt to address these lines to you, having been away from home a great deal and having never been over-demonstrative in my nature. I scarcely expected on leaving, my dear family, to feel as I do now, for the last few days. I more fully realize what a great strong bond of union I am now separating from, and the thought that it may be forever, very nearly overcomes me, for I feel that I am fast losing strength, appetite, memory, and probably judgment to some extent. And the thought of President A. K. Thurber and others who have passed away stepping out of the reach of persecution so easily of late, that it begins to appear to me that it is only

31. Ibid., p. 195.

a short step and our troubles are all at an end and Eternity opens to our view.

"This I mean of course is wherein our Heavenly Father so orders it. But one thing I can say: that I am not afraid of anything unless it be to disobey the commandments of God, and while I feel this way I desire to warn you, my dear wives and children, that the great day of trial for the Saints is at our very doors, and Satan has great power and will make many believe that it is not worth while to keep up the struggle for Truth and righteousness; but that we can sin a little in gratifying our appetites and bodily passions, that we will only be beaten with a few stripes and then the Lord will forgive and all will be well. But, my dear ones, I desire that you will all remember the late revelation of the Lord to President John Taylor, wherein he declares that—'Hereafter, He will not honor or acknowledge any longer those who bear His Holy Priesthood and do not honor and acknowledge Him.' And now let me say to my sons, that you cannot drink strong drink, play pool, or gamble in any way, or swear, and neglect every duty, and continue to hold the Melchizedek Priesthood and still be blest of the Lord. His holy spirit will cease to strive with you and you will meet with troubles and sorrows in days to come, in abundance. Your parents have honored their covenants to their best ability and you are legal heirs of salvation, but if you sin in these things, you will be shut out from the Lord until repentance comes and full restitution is made; for any degree of unholiness cannot be admitted where the righteous dwell in Eternity. It is an easy matter to attend to your family prayers every night and morning, and I feel sure that your good wives and mothers will help you to do this, and after performing this duty sincerely, you will not feel like going to the pool hall and listening to the evil conversations and partake of the influences of the saloon and its surroundings. The society of your own families will have charms that are found nowhere else. You will find that the Lord will grant you more of his holy spirit when you acknowledge him twice in twenty-four hours.

"And now let me say to all of you that the Lord requires more sacrifice and more integrity to principle to sustain His work. Perfect honesty and truthfulness will have its reward. No matter what your next door neighbor is doing, let us do right.

"Now, dear children, both sons and daughters, I speak to all. I pray you to remember your duties to the Lord daily, and you will truly be supported in your various trials and adverse visitations, for we must all be tried and tested. Strive to be an honor to your parents and your callings, and if we should never meet again on this earth, I shall be satisfied to be able to welcome you all in the realms above.

"My prayer is that you may be continually faithful and not fall into evil ways, but always set a good example to your younger brothers who now hold the lesser Priesthood, and if all those boys will continue to attend their Quorum meetings and perform all duties that belong to their several callings, they will grow in usefulness and integrity and yet become bright and shining lights in the kingdom of God.

"And I will further say that you will no doubt hear your father evil spoken of in these times of trial which cannot be helped, but this I desire to say, that I have not intentionally wronged any person that I know of, but am as liable to make mistakes as others, and wherein claims are made in my absence that appear to be pressing, just please take counsel together and do what you find to be right; and here let me plead with you to be untied as a family and be forgiving and lovable towards each other, and you will find an increase of the good spirit in your hearts. I can assure you that I have the best of feelings towards you all, and including my sons-in-law and daughters-in-law, wives, children, and grandchildren, and—In the name of Jesus Christ and by the Authority of the Holy Priesthood invested in me, I do bless you in all your works of righteousness that you may continue to be fruitful and multiply and have abundance of the good things of this life and an eternal inheritance in the worlds to come, Amen.

"P.S.—I hope that you will not neglect about New Year's, to have a Family meeting of all within reach and encourage each other in well doing. Let your influence be felt for good, for there is plenty of evil about us. May the Lord preserve you all, is my constant prayer.

George W. Bean"[32]

Three months later, in March 1889, George joyously returned home to his family. Scarcely three weeks later, he was confronted by a deputy marshal on his doorstep with a warrant for his arrest for polygamy. George's three wives and four of his children were requested to attend as his witnesses in the Provo trial.

Having worked in courts officially for many years serving as Superior Court Judge in the State of Utah, state legislator, U. S. Deputy Marshal and tax assessor, George knew the process of law. He and his family passed through the preliminaries without incident. Seeing how other trials humiliated the participants, George was determined not to put his loved ones through that kind of ordeal. With the scripture in mind, "Take no thought of what ye shall say," etc., he proceeded without a lawyer and plead guilty to the crime of "cohabitation."[33]

Bishop John E. Booth, Attorney at Law, arose and addressed the court in George's defense. In the words of the accused:

"He recited, in graphic language, the trials and hardships of this man in crossing the plains with his ox teams in 1847,

32. Ibid., p. 199-201.
33. Ibid., p. 203.

and as a Utah Pioneer, aged 16, who helped to build the first two Forts in Utah, in Salt Lake City and Provo; had been a Guide and Indian Interpreter for State and Government Officials; had risked his life many times in teaching the Indians and assisting in their Treaties; had held many offices in City and County; had been U. S. Deputy Marshal when danger lurked at every turn; had been Prosecuting Attorney in the District Court and done much civic work, etc., and was Judge in this County when this Court House in which you are holding Court was built."[34]

He proceeded to point out that George had done all his marrying as early as 1856 before there was a law prohibiting it. Judge Judd, who was presiding in the courtroom, said, "Mr. Bean, this Law was not made for cases like yours, but you have been indicted and plead guilty. Therefore the case must be disposed of. I fine you fifty dollars, and hope you will return home and continue to be a good citizen."[35]

George paid additional court fees totaling $315.45 on that never-to-be-forgotten afternoon of October 11, 1889. Others convicted of this "heinous" crime paid considerably more and were forced to spend long periods of time behind bars in their striped suits of black and white.

President Wilford Woodruff and other church leaders realized how critical the situation was and issued a "Manifesto" abolishing the practice of plural marriage in 1890.

From this Parentage. . .

In his lifetime, George had been personally acquainted with four presidents of The Church of Jesus Christ of Latter-day Saints—Joseph Smith, Brigham Young, John Taylor and Wilford Woodruff. He was an avid reader of the Bible, having read it from cover to cover seven times, and could ably lecture on its contents. He was

34. Ibid.
35. Ibid., p. 204.

ordained a High Priest in 1877 and set apart as First Counselor to President Seegmiller of the Sevier Stake by Apostle John W. Taylor on May 27, 1888. He served in that position almost six years before being ordained a Patriarch by Apostle John Henry Smith in August 1893.

George's first wife, Elizabeth, was called to be Stake Relief Society President in the Sevier Stake under the direction of the General Relief Society President, Eliza R. Snow. Elizabeth served in that position for twenty years.

Elizabeth earned the reputation of being one of the finest farmers in the county and harvested and preserved much of the family's food. George recorded: "Our boys said that Mother preserved everything when we killed hogs, but the squeal, and they tried to save that."[36]

Elizabeth was a skilled weaver, designer and seamstress. All the children, boys and girls alike, wore "homespun."

From this parentage came Willard Washington Bean—a man endowed with a respect for law and order; a scriptorian who could "quote scriptures until the cows come home;"[37] a man willing, capable, and eager to work and care for the needs of his family; a man totally devoted to the gospel of Jesus Christ.

---

36. Ibid., p. 245.
37. Ibid., p. 253.

Rebecca and Willard Bean
February 14, 1915

PALMYRA REVISITED

The Call to Palmyra

Apostle George Albert Smith took every opportunity to visit the William Avery Chapman family on the Joseph Smith Farm when he traveled east. He struck up a friendship with the family that owned the farm in the hope that someday Mr. Chapman would agree to sell the property to the Church.

That dream was realized in 1907. Elder Smith arranged for the purchase of the home but had to wait another seven years before the Chapmans actually left the farm and turned it completely over to the Church.

President Joseph F. Smith was then faced with the problem of finding a suitable family to send to Palmyra, New York, to live in the Joseph Smith home. He knew it would have to be a fighting man for the prejudice was severe in Joseph's old home town. Yet the man would have to be friendly, patient, loving and have unsurpassed knowledge of the gospel. Such a man was found in Willard Bean.

Willard and Rebecca Peterson Bean were living in Richfield, Utah, having married in the Manti Temple just a few months earlier on September 18, 1914. Of his new bride, Willard recorded in his journal:

"She was of good old Scandinavian stock, comely appearance, wholesome countenance, socially popular, of good reputation, domestically inclined, extremely practical with sterling qualities, active in church work, one of the leading sopranos in the ward choir, etc. All these qualities appealed to me. She also saw qualities in me that appealed to her, or at least could tolerate, and a pleasant courtship got underway."[1]

President Joseph F. Smith and Apostle George Albert Smith presided over the stake conference in Richfield which the newlyweds attended. Rebecca was sitting in the choir seats as Willard entered the side door of the chapel. Rebecca gave this account of what happened next:

> "The minute he stepped in, President Smith stood up and said, 'Would Willard Bean please come to the stand.' As they met, he said, 'Willard, I've got another mission for you. After this service is over, I'll tell you all about it.' President Smith later said, 'When Willard stepped in that door, the impression was so strong it was just like a voice said to me, "There's your man."'

> "And that's how we were called to go back to Palmyra. That's how we were called to the place where holy men have walked, the place where God with man has talked, and where our prophet lived for 15 years, where he suffered much persecution, and where he lived and loved as a young man."[2]

In the springtime of 1915, President Joseph F. Smith set Willard and Rebecca apart to go to Palmyra for "five years or longer." They were warned that they would find it the most prejudiced place in the world. President Smith said, "Willard, knowing you and your missionary work and your fighting spirit, I'm sure you are the right man to send."[3]

The Beans arrived in Palmyra in February of 1915, and the townspeople were waiting for them. To say they were unwelcome

---

1. Bean, Autobiography, p. 102.
2. Bean tape recording.
3. Ibid.

would be a gross understatement. The venom fairly seeped from their beings. Mormons hadn't lived in Palmyra for 84 years. The saints had been driven out by angry mobs in 1831, and the fathers passed on to their children an intense hatred for anyone associated with "Old Joe Smith."

The Beans soon learned that not only would the townsfolk not speak to them or wait on them in the stores, but they would pull their dogs away from them and cross to the other side of the street to avoid any semblance of contact. For a number of years, they were forced to drive their horse and buggy to neighboring towns just to buy groceries. Vindictive passersby paused long enough in front of their home to scream obscenities and vehemently suggest that they go back to Utah where they came from. Some were so bold as to come to their door calling them vile names and insisting they leave their community.

One evening a short time after the Beans had settled into their new home, a knock came at the door. Willard opened it to find three men standing on the porch.

"Won't you come in?" Willard offered.

"No, Mr. Bean," was their reply. "You step outside. We've held a meeting tonight and we're here to tell you people to leave Palmyra. We don't want any Mormons here."

"Now, I'm sorry to hear that," replied Willard in typical unflappable form. "We had hoped to come out here and fit in with you people and be an asset to this community. But I'm telling you, we're here to stay if we have to fight our way. I'll take you on one at a time or three at a time. We're here to stay."[4]

Though the men were unaware of his prowess as a fighter, they somehow sensed his sincerity. The committee fled and nothing more was ever heard from them.

---

4. Ibid.

Willard Bean was a determined man. Their call had been to go to Palmyra and live in the Joseph Smith home for not less than five years. The end result was a 25-year legacy. They went to New York as newlyweds and returned to their home in Salt Lake City as grandparents. The Beans made a mark on that small town that would not soon be forgotten.

The Lay of the Land

The Smith Farm in Palmyra, New York, consisted of 155 acres. One hundred thirty-five acres were in the township of Manchester, Ontario County. The remaining twenty acres were in Palmyra, Wayne County. The farm was located on the borderline of both counties.

Though most farms specialized in just one or two kinds of crops, the small farms in New York were known to produce a bit of everything. When Willard and Rebecca Bean occupied the home, they raised all kinds of grains, wheat, barley, oats and beans. They cultivated twenty to thirty acres of peas every year. Acres of cabbage and celery were grown on their land as well. They harvested everything and kept it in their own barns before selling what they didn't need for themselves and their livestock.

A variety of animals were kept on the farm. The Beans had a dairy herd of 17 to 20 cows. They had 12 to 15 horses which were used primarily for farming purposes due to the absence of tractors and heavy farming equipment in those days. They had sheep, hundreds of chickens, geese, ducks and guinea hens. Even wild pheasants came down in the winter to eat with their chickens.

An assortment of ducks enjoyed swimming in the creek across the road from the house. Ducks often walk single file, and when a procession of 75 to 100 of them started across the road, nothing could stop them. People driving down the road in cars or buggies simply had to wait it out—which was known to be as long as 15 minutes. When the geese decided to follow along, it turned into a great lesson in patience for unsuspecting motorists.

PALMYRA REVISITED

The Beans butchered their own meat, canned their own vegetables and preserved most of their own food. The winters were so cold, the meat could be stored in an upstairs room over the woodshed and would stay frozen all winter. Apples were stored in big bins surrounded by straw to keep them from freezing.

The Bean children—Palmyra, Alvin Pliny (who was known as Pliny until he left home for college at the age of 18), Dawn and Kelvin—loved to lay on the bank of the creek that ran through the farm. They would watch the minnows, tadpoles, frogs and turtles as they played in the water. Many of the turtles were snapping turtles—much to the distress of the ducks swimming by. Often a turtle would snap off the foot of a passing duck and the poor creature would hobble back onto dry land on one foot with just a stump where its other leg had been. That duck was destined to be eaten for dinner the following Sunday.

Only a few turkeys were raised on the farm while the Beans lived there. Thanksgiving and Christmas dinners usually featured ducks or geese. The African geese raised there were huge—up to twenty pounds. They provided as much meat as a turkey for special occasions.

During the winter, the three boys trapped muskrats and weasels along the creek. The mischievous lads even trapped an occasional skunk. Willard taught his sons how to skin the animals and stretch the hides. All went well until they skinned a skunk in the woodshed and stretched the hide on a board. It took quite a while for the smell to dissipate, and the boys earned only 50¢ for the hide and all their work.

Cars and trucks and raceways were not available in stores in those days. Young boys had to learn to be creative. The Bean children played in the clay deposits at the end of the barn. The earth around the barn was very hard clay; and when it rained, as it did very often in Palmyra, the clay became soft and pliable. The children dug the clay out with their fingers and molded their playthings—trucks, cars, horses, wagons, people. The clay objects were set in the sun to harden. Their masterpieces were then transported to a sandy spot next to the road where streets and villages could be constructed. Of course, when it rained again, the sand would wash away and the roads and clay would dissolve; but what fun they had creating it all over again.

The Bean children were taught to work at a very young age. Almost as soon as they were old enough to walk, the boys were given the assignment of gathering the cows home every night. When they were a little older, they helped milk them. The milking chores had to be done about 4:30 in the morning in the summer because as soon as the sun came up the cows had to be taken to the field before the boys could continue with their other farm work.

Rebecca sent her youngsters out along the fence lines to pick wild berries. A variety of berries grew in great abundance along the stone wall at the foot of the hill that ran behind the Smith home. (That was the fence the prophet Joseph was climbing when he came back from the field the morning after his visitations from the Angel Moroni. The Angel appeared to him again as he climbed the fence, giving him the same instructions he had given the night before.) There are many stone fences in that area because as the land was cleared, the accumulation of stones was used to build walls. Sometimes entire houses (known as cobble rock houses) were built from these stones.

Packs of wild dogs caused considerable excitement in the Palmyra area. The dogs seemed to derive great satisfaction from attacking sheep—not to eat them but just for the thrill of the kill. They would kill as many as twenty sheep in one night. When a rustling was heard among the animals in the night, Willard would get up and grab his gun. Young Alvin was anxious to help and would throw on his overalls and go with his father as often as he was allowed. They dashed out with guns blazing. If their bullets didn't find their mark, they were at least successful in scaring the dogs away. It was not uncommon to engage in this nocturnal activity as often as two or three times a week during certain times of the year.

PALMYRA REVISITED

Early baptisms in Palmyra were performed in the creek that ran behind the barn. That same creek was used for baptisms when Joseph Smith lived there. Palmyra, Rebecca and Willard's oldest child, was the first in the family to be baptized there. She was followed by her three younger brothers as they each reached the age of eight. Palmyra was confirmed by Apostle James E. Talmage who was a frequent visitor to the farm. President Heber J. Grant was also present on that occasion.

One problem that never existed for the people baptized in the creek was that of having their feet or toes float up out of the water. The creek was dammed up the day before a baptism to create a deep pool. Because of the muddy bottom, baptism candidates sank into the mire up to their knees. No one's feet came up at all!

To cause further problems, a person entering the water riled up the mud. They had to wait for the sediment to float away before performing the baptism. It was several years before a concrete font was built in Palmyra.

In 40° below zero winter weather, the children traveled two miles to school by bobsled. Some snowdrifts were so deep, the youngsters could easily step over the telephone wires. The snow was so deep between the house and the chicken coop, the Beans had to dig a tunnel thirty to forty feet long to provide a passageway to feed the chickens, ducks, geese and turkeys and gather the eggs. The kids thought that was great sport. The tunnel remained until the first thaw.

The Bean family used wood for heating and cooking. In the fall of the year, they cut down trees and sawed them with a tractor and buzz saw to put wood away for the winter. Trees in the Sacred Grove were never cut down, nor was the Grove used for a pasture. It was allowed to grow in its natural state unhindered by the insensitivities of man.

Like most of the city's citizens, the Bean family traveled by horse and buggy. Willard had been a cowboy part of his life and was an expert at dealing with wild horses. He wasn't concerned about taming them too much. He used them no matter what their disposition. Willard was known to secure his wife and children in the buggy seat and hitch a single wild pony to the front of the buggy. He would release the rearing horse's head, take one leap over the front of the buggy and land in the seat beside his family. The horse was almost up to full speed before Willard hit the seat.

Not only did this cowboy have a fetish for wild horses, but he also loved wild bulls. The Beans had a bull that captured first prize at the county fair every year. They kept a ring in its nose attached to a ten-foot chain as well as a long chain fastened to its foot to keep it from charging through gates or fences or whatever else seemed to echo a call to the wild.

One day while changing the ring in the bull's nose, the animal broke loose and gored Willard badly. With predictable determination, Willard rolled around a tree until he had a chance to get up. Not willing to let the bull get the best of him, Willard and a hired hand threw the bull down again and finished attaching the ring to its nose. Content that he had won the battle, Willard collapsed from loss of blood. Young Alvin helped carry his father into the house. A doctor was summoned, but it was four or five hours before medical help arrived. Willard's life was miraculously spared.

A similar experience happened with one of the family's boar pigs. It, too, was a prize-winning specimen sporting tusks ten inches long. It developed a vengeance for Willard one day and ripped up one side of his leg. The gash was severe and Willard was furious. He jumped over the fence, got a crowbar from the barn and returned to beat the tusks off the boar. After putting the crowbar back in the barn, he hobbled to the house to call a doctor.

The Bean children learned to be missionaries and guides at a very early age. They escorted visitors to the Sacred Grove, Hill Cumorah and Martin Harris farm as early as five years of age. They took guests through the house where Joseph Smith lived and detailed the story of what transpired there. Many times visitors offered the children a nickel or dime for their efforts. Their first tithing was paid on these tips received for taking people to the historical sites of the church. (As a pre-schooler, Alvin was known to ask for a dime when offered a nickel because he didn't know how to take 10% of a nickel!)

The children were often slow to retire to bed after being sent upstairs in the evening. They developed great testimonies as they listened to the conversations below between mother and dad and the church authorities. Some of the most memorable stories they overheard on those occasions were about Willard's mission in Tennessee in the 1890s—the dangers and persecution he suffered there as well as the triumphs and spiritual blessings of serving in that ominous territory.

When Alvin was about four years old, he helped his father put new barbed wire around a pasture near the Hill Cumorah. A man, large in stature, came along and began to ridicule the Mormons. As the filthy names and accusations continued, Willard's tolerance grew scarce. Exasperated, he put down his hammer and said, "I've heard just about enough. Do you want to leave now while you're able or do you want to spend the rest of the day on your back?"[5]

The husky gentleman was feeling pretty cocky and decided to pursue it. Willard took one step and made contact. The intruder was knocked out cold. Willard picked up his hammer and casually continued stringing the barbed wire. The man came to about 15 minutes later and, embarrassed and bewildered, slunk away.

Alvin was six years old and entering the first grade when he started school in Palmyra in 1924. On presenting himself to the teacher, he was escorted to a desk which had been screwed to the floor in the back corner of the room. Several students had brought notes from their parents stating that they did not want their children sitting next to "that Mormon boy" who was coming

5.   Alvin Pliny Bean fireside address, November 5, 1978. Tape recording and transcript in possession of Vicki Bean Topliff, Orem, Utah. (Hereafter cited as Alvin Bean Transcript.)

to school. Thus he was relegated to a lonely corner and shunned by the other boys and girls in his class.

For several weeks he sat by himself until it became more embarrassing for the teacher and the other students than it was for Alvin. One morning he arrived at school to find that his desk had been moved back over in the regular row of chairs.

The Bean children suffered considerable harassment at school for a number of years. Other students took delight in stealing their lunches and hiding their galoshes. The teachers were not at all sympathetic, so the Mormon children were on their own to suffer the mistreatment.

As the years went on, things began to change. The children participated in school activities and excelled in athletics. All four were bright students and got outstanding grades. Palmyra was the valedictorian of her graduating class. (Alvin contends that he would have been, too, if it weren't for the fact that all the smart kids were in his class!)

A Nurse was Needed

When Rebecca was expecting her first child, she contacted several nurses in an effort to find one willing to stay in the home and assist when the baby was born. Every nurse contacted gave the same reply—they wouldn't go into a Mormon home.

"I worried about it and prayed about it," said Rebecca, "and one day a lady came to my door. She lived on a farm not too far from us."

"I understand you can't get a nurse to come and stay with you when your baby comes," said the stranger.

"No," Rebecca answered, "and I've contacted several."

"I'm not a trained nurse," the woman admitted, "but I've helped in a lot of cases like this, and I'm not afraid to come. My brother went to Salt Lake City just for curiosity, and he liked it so well he stayed out there. He told me that all the awful things he'd heard were lies, and I'm willing to take my brother's word for it."[6]

The woman stayed with the Beans for three weeks after their little girl was born. Rebecca and Willard named their new daughter Palmyra.

Someone Stood Beside Me

The Bean family lived with prejudice for a long time. Rebecca especially dreaded answering the door because so often she would be met with obscenities and irreverent remarks about the Mormons. "Go home. We don't want you here,"[7] was not an uncommon greeting as people passed their home.

One afternoon while Willard was in town, a knock came at the door. Rebecca, holding her 10-month-old daughter in her arms, hesitated. The visitor was persistent and kept ringing the bell until she warily opened the door. The porch was covered with men, and they had five ladies with them.

"We're ministers," they announced, "and these ladies are school teachers. We've been over to Clifton Springs to attend a ministerial convention. We passed Mormon Hill and thought we'd come over and see this place and hear a little about old Joe Smith."[8]

Rebecca thought it strange how everyone spoke of the prophet as "Old Joe Smith" when he was such a young man. She concluded that they must have thought they insulted him a little more if they referred to him in that manner.

Rebecca gave this account of what transpired next:

"I invited them in, and I had my little baby in my arms. I started to tell them that this was the room where the prophet brought the plates and hid them under the hearth-

6. Bean tape recording.
7. Ibid.
8. Ibid.

stone. I pointed out the spot where the fireplace had been and where the hearthstone would be, but that's as far as I got. They just started yelling and screaming questions at me, never waiting for an answer, and it was just terrible.

"My little baby just cried and was frightened, and I have never had a feeling like that in me in my whole life. I felt I had to pray, and I wondered how I could pray in a situation like that. But I did. I prayed deep down inside of me without saying a word. And then all at once a haze came into the room. It was so quiet and so different. And then I felt like someone stood beside me.

"I bear humble testimony that after that I knew the Prophet Joseph Smith. I was able to go on and tell Joseph's story and defend him and tell about his receiving the plates, and they listened. They didn't say anything anymore. When I was through talking, I asked them if they'd like to go upstairs and see the room where the Angel Moroni had come to the Prophet Joseph. They all followed me upstairs. When we came down, I asked them if they'd like to register in the book where we had our visitors write their names, and they did. One or two of them apologized for their behavior and thanked me for what I had told them. Then they went outside.

"I sat down in my rocker. My little baby had dropped off to sleep, and I sat down and meditated over what had happened—this wonderful feeling that had come into the room and the knowledge and feeling that someone stood beside me to help me. And again I say, after that I knew the Prophet Joseph Smith, and I felt his love and his influence all the years we lived there. Even my little children felt it. To us he was Joseph. When they spoke of him, they spoke his name tenderly. They grew up learning about the things that happened there. They could take anybody through the house; they could take them to the Grove; they could take them to the Hill and tell them all about it. They talked about it just like grown people did, and it had become a great part of their lives."[9]

Anti-Mormons Imported

The ministers of Palmyra concluded one day that something needed to be done to check the influence of Willard Bean in their community. They called for "old Reverend Nutting who once toured Utah in a reduced-sized sheep wagon peddling his stuff."[10] This plan of attack backfired. After his first lecture, the ministers decided his name should be changed to Nutty instead of Nutting.

Next the over-zealous ministers contacted the Christian Reform Association at Pittsburgh, Pennsylvania, to supply character assassins to combat Mormonism. The Association sent Mrs. Lulu Loveland Shepherd, well-known in Utah and quite a melodramatic actress.

It is unnecessary to quote her slanderous harangue of abuse; but when she made a return visit three weeks later, she followed an entirely new line of thought. She brought with her a male companion whom she called her bodyguard. Lulu told the townspeople that she had received many threatening letters from the Mormons and that her life was in danger. She couldn't sleep nights fearing someone was stalking her. She was haunted with dreams. One night she saw a man standing over her with a broad-bladed ax in his hand; and just as he was bringing it down to sever her head, she screamed and sat up in bed.

"Since then I have taken a bodyguard along," Lulu dramatized, "which means that my traveling expenses have been doubled—an extra fare traveling and at hotels and restaurants. But I feel confident that you good people will be liberal with your contributions."[11]

9. Ibid.
10. Bean, Autobiography, p. 107.
11. Ibid., p. 108.

Lulu went on to tell the people that there was a polygamist in their midst who had not only two wives but three! (When Willard arrived in Palmyra with a young wife and two children from an earlier marriage, the townspeople accepted that as indisputable proof that he was a polygamist. It only served to amuse Willard who had endured far worse persecution as a missionary in Tennessee.)

Lulu was succeeded in her Satanic quest by a Dr. Dodge who had been granted three months leave of absence from his ministry so he could "devote his time unhindered to this hydro-headed monster called Mormonism."[12] He was followed by Attorney Alexander, an apostate Mormon from Independence, Missouri, and Mrs. Walker, a teacher from Utah.

The ministers of four churches—Presbyterian, Methodist, Baptist and Dutch Reform—planned and carried on this ignominious fight to check the Latter-day Saints in Palmyra. The Catholic and Episcopal refused to take part.

Willard decided it was time to make his move. He requested permission to occupy a Presbyterian chapel to "give the other side of the question." He added, "I am willing to personally pay all the expenses and take up no collections."[13]

Reverend Wright stood so full of anger, he could scarcely contain himself. He pounded the pulpit and thundered, "The idea of a polygamist Mormon asking for the privilege of occupying a Christian pulpit. The very thought is preposterous. We did not build our churches for Mormon propaganda. We would not have pulpits disgraced by letting a Mormon stand in them. My answer is an emphatic NO!"[14]

The reverend was too strong. His venom left a nauseating stench the congregation smelled and felt. A short time later, when the prejudice cleared away, he was the first one asked to hand in his resignation.

12. Ibid.
13. Ibid.
14. Ibid., p. 109.

Street Meetings

Willard decided the time had come to "open up our batteries and start an aggressive defense."[15] He rented a hall and delivered a series of lectures. Even local ministers attended the meetings. Townspeople began inviting the Beans to their homes. Cottage meetings were held, and soon converts were brought into the church.

Willard began holding street meetings at the main intersection of town. Saturday night was alive with farmers migrating to the city to trade their produce for groceries and other goods. There wasn't much to do in the small town of Palmyra besides go to the local theater (10¢ a show) or to the ice cream parlor for a 5¢ cone or 10¢ sundae. The street meetings proved to be a welcome alternative.

Willard laid his Bible and Book of Mormon on an apple crate and attracted attention by singing. "Mrs. Bean was a good soprano, and I could make a noise,"[16] he was known to say.

Soon a convert was made who could play the violin, and together they made beautiful music. Willard had the voice of a bull moose and could be herd all over town when he started preaching. Invariably a large crowd gathered.

Eventually complaints rolled in that the missionaries were blockading traffic. This turned out to be to their advantage as Willard approached Pliny Sexton, the local banker, asking permission to preach in the lovely and spacious park adjoining his bank. Mr. Sexton not only granted that privilege but went a step further by offering his bandstand for a pulpit and the use of his park lights. In that setting, 200 to 400 curious observers gathered when Willard began to preach.

After a few years, the Beans became the proud owners of a Graham Page Touring Car with a spotlight clipped to the side of the windshield. While Willard preached on one occasion, preco-

---

15. Ibid.
16. Ibid.

cious Alvin entertained himself by playing with the car spotlight. He flashed it on a building across the street from the park. A man in the audience, feeling the spirit, suddenly began to cry, "I see the light. I see the light." He really believed he had seen a light from heaven. Willard looked up, stopped mid-sentence and said, "Son, shut off the spotlight." With that, he went right on preaching as if nothing had happened.[17]

Though many people in Palmyra were slow to accept the gospel, they obviously didn't discount everything the Mormon's had to say. Very often a myriad of tiny lights could be seen on the Hill Cumorah late at night. Those lights were lanterns belonging to people who were on the hill with their picks and shovels digging for the gold the Mormons told them existed there in the form of golden plates. Of course, no one ever found it, but the Beans took great delight in watching them try. The hill was pock-marked with holes for a number of years.

The Golden Plates Hoax

Just when the Beans thought the anti-Mormon fever had abated, another outbreak appeared. The minister of the Church of God announced that he would expose Mormonism the following Sunday claiming that he had in his possession absolute proof that the "Mormon Bible" (Book of Mormon) was a hoax. He produced for the anxious congregation three pieces of tin but refused to allow anyone the opportunity of examining them. The Rochester newspapers gave the story elaborate coverage, and within a few days reporters were in town to learn the facts.

Evangelists told the story that they were on the Hill Cumorah when they came upon a spot that attracted their attention. They felt impressed to investigate. Three plates containing Latin characters were unearthed.

---

17. Alvin Bean transcript, p. 13.

The newspaper reporters requested the privilege of scrutinizing and photographing the plates. On doing so, they quickly discerned their true origin. The plates were cut with tinner's shears from a sheet of common gutter tin—obviously freshly cut. A common punch had been used to make a few Latin characters. One of the reporters, a friend of Willard's, told him of the clumsy counterfeit and they enjoyed a hearty laugh.

The consequence: The local minister lost his job and left the village. The loud-mouthed Evangelist made a hit with the local congregation and was installed as their spiritual advisor. He sent for his wife and daughter, and all went well for a while. Eventually his popularity waned. His wife died and his 12-year-old daughter took over the household and other duties. He continued his ministerial duties until, without any announcement, he and his daughter mysteriously disappeared. They were later heard to be in New Jersey where the daughter was in a maternity home. Her child's father proved to be her father. The ill-fated minister who planned the gutter tin plate hoax was sent to the penitentiary to do penance for twenty years.

Rivalry in Print

In a street meeting, Willard made the remark: "One of the greatest joys that can come to me after I get into the spirit world will be to preach the gospel to these character assassins and Mormon maligners in hell."[18]

A local minister, Reverend Martin, took exception to Willard's statement and sent an article to the local newspaper regarding it. Willard replied through the newspaper offering to occupy the minister's pulpit and answer any questions to his entire satisfaction.

---

18. Bean, Autobiography, p. 110.

The reverend ignored his reply and entered another article in the paper. This went on for days and several more articles were exchanged until Willard finally wrote the following:

> "Reverend Martin, for some reason, continues to ignore my propositions. I shall try one more. I will rent the Odd Fellows hall next Sunday afternoon when I shall endeavor to answer his questions. I shall personally bear all the expenses and give Reverend Martin the privilege of replying after I get through. Accordingly, I cordially invite Reverend Martin and his congregation, and others who may be interested, to be present. I shall take up no collection."[19]

A large congregation gathered, but Reverend Martin was conspicuous by his absence. During the following week, the reverend took yet another article to the newspaper office. He met with a newspaper manager who was not impressed by his behavior.

"Mr. Bean has made you every proposition a reasonable man could ask for," he began. "You started this controversy with Mr. Bean, but you haven't got the guts to back up your accusations. Better take your article home. If you leave it here, I shall consign it to the waste basket."[20]

Reverend Martin's declining popularity soon made it necessary for him to be released from his ministerial post. Before he left, Willard entered one last article in Palmyra's newspaper. It read:

> "I did not come to Palmyra to fight other churches or any man because of his religion or lack of religion. I am naturally a tolerant and peaceable man and hoped to fit in with the better element and work for the moral uplift and betterment of the community. But I have a little fighting blood in my veins, and when I or my people are maliciously attacked by character assassins, I feel it my privilege and duty to fight back in self defense. And may I suggest that in the future if

19. Ibid., p. 111.
20. Ibid.

any of the ministers feel the urge to expose my religion it is not necessary for them to send away for a group of paid hirelings to expose Mormonism, so-called. Remember that I will gladly do it without cost."[21]

There were but a few more incidents of anti-Mormons attempting to defame the church. A few more debates were scheduled, but, oddly enough, the opposing speakers were always called out of town a day or two before the debate. The battle for survival was finally won, but the climate in town still left much to be desired.

The Boxing Exhibition

Being the fun-loving athlete that he was and in an effort to break through the icy reception the family was still receiving in some circles, Willard offered to put on a boxing exhibition. A ring was constructed in the old opera house in the middle of town. The confident fighter-preacher challenged anybody in the community to get in the ring with him.

The night of the exhibition arrived. On the first three rows sat the biggest bruisers in the community. The time came to start and the first one climbed into the ring. Opponent #1 didn't even get to land a blow. He lasted less than 15 seconds. He was carried out of the ring and the second aspirant entered. He, too, was carried out within a matter of seconds. This went on until the seventh would-be pugilist was carried from the arena. Not one had lasted a round. The eighth man declined the invitation to join his opponent, and no more takers could be found.

Almost as humiliating as losing the match in the first 15 seconds of the round was the fact that Willard, an outstanding gymnast as well as boxer, would do a back flip in the air and a few other gymnastic stunts while the bodies of his opponents were being carried from the arena.

---

21. Ibid.

To continue the competition a bit further, Willard took a piece of chalk and drew a two-foot circle in the middle of the ring. He challenged anyone in the audience to knock him out of the circle. Many tried but not one succeeded.

The exhibition was a success, and people became more friendly. They gained respect for Willard and his family even though they had suffered some embarrassment in the process.

Willard continued to give exhibitions in boxing and tumbling. To the youngsters delight, he demonstrated how he could kill a fly on the wall with his boxing gloves, and the sound of the glove hitting the wall was totally indiscernible. The fact was, he was so fast and accurate, his glove never touched the wall!

Willard gave his own boys boxing lessons but never encouraged them to go into the game professionally. This wise father gave this counsel: "Now, son, never pick a fight, but you're going to get in some. When you do, you want to make believe the man's face is a foot further away than it really is."[22]

The resulting impact was staggering. Practical experience proved Willard's advice to be worth remembering.

Children and adults alike delighted in watching this agile athlete perform. He could run across the road and leap over a team of horses without touching a hair. He would run out the kitchen door and jump a five-foot wire fence just for exercise. His body was in excellent physical condition, and he could accomplish such feats well into his old age.

Attended Many Churches

Willard and his family visited a variety of churches during their years on the farm. Being exceptionally well-versed in the scriptures, Willard eloquently quoted and interpreted many passages in Bible classes that even the teachers were unable to explain. The

---

22. Alvin Bean transcript, p. 25.

instructors enjoyed having him participate, but he was careful to answer questions only when asked so as not to upset members of the congregation.

Since no LDS branch or ward had been organized as yet, Willard began taking part in the Baptist Sunday School lessons. At the end of class, the teacher consistently turned to Willard to say: "And now, Mr. Bean, we haven't heard from you yet."[23] Willard proceeded to quote scripture bearing on the lesson without comment, letting the people place their own interpretation on it. The class expected it and enjoyed it, but jealousy began to rear its ugly head and some super-pious members began to fear lest Willard gain too much influence with the young people.

It wasn't until the deacons of the church visited members to collect pledges that Willard offered to withdraw his attendance from the Baptist church. Two multi-millionaire heiresses refused to give their financial support to the church as long as "that Mormon polygamist took active part,"[24] so Willard felt it only fair to make himself scarce until the smoke cleared.

When word reached the Presbyterian minister that Willard was no longer attending the Baptist church, he quickly telephoned and asked him to attend their meetings. Willard gladly consented. Again, he was helpful in explaining many scriptures that other church leaders were at a loss to interpret. It wasn't long, however, before jealousy surfaced once again and Willard deemed it advisable to worship elsewhere.

James Talmage, a Dear Friend

Apostle James E. Talmage, a member of the Quorum of Twelve Apostles, was a dear friend of the Bean family and visited the Smith farm often. He was with the saints for conference when Palmyra Bean was to be baptized.

23. Bean, Autobiography, p. 104.
24. Ibid.

Hundreds of people were present for the conference. The stream behind the barn had been dammed up to create a pool for the baptisms that were to take place that Saturday.

Rebecca caught Dr. Talmage alone and said, "I'd like my little daughter to be confirmed by you. I think that would be something lovely for her to remember, and I would be so pleased with it."

Dr. Talmage smiled at Rebecca and said, "President Grant is in charge of the meeting. I hate to make any suggestions, but let's you and I pray about it." That was all he said.

The next day all those who had been baptized were confirmed. Rebecca was pleased when it was Palmyra's turn to be seated in front, and she was even more thrilled when President Heber J. Grant said, "I think we'll have Dr. Talmage confirm little Palmyra Bean."[25] Dr. Talmage smiled at Rebecca as he passed her. She knew he had prayed about it—and she had too.

Dr. Talmage visited on another occasion when a conference was being held in the Sacred Grove. After the conference was over, those who were staying with the Beans went home, ate dinner and retired to bed. Three or four hours passed and Dr. Talmage still hadn't returned from the Grove. Willard lit a lantern and went to find him.

As he entered the Grove, Willard could hear the sound of footsteps. "I was afraid you might have gotten turned around in the grove and were unable to find your way out," he said as they met.

"No, Brother Bean," said Dr. Talmage, "I was just on my way out now." And then he haltingly remarked, "The things I have seen and heard this day. . . ."

The two went back to the house where Dr. Talmage requested just bread and milk for supper. After eating, he said, "Willard, get me the Bible and the Book of Mormon." He read some passages of scripture to those seated around him.

---

25. Bean tape recording.

"I guess we'll read some of your experiences today in the Deseret News, won't we?" said Willard.

Dr. Talmage's reply was precise. "Brother Bean, when I tell the authorities what I have seen and heard this day, I'm sure they won't want to print it." And then he added,

"My poor, poor people."[26]

A Visit with the Savior

Ole Peterson and Julia Hansen joined the church in Denmark in 1868. They sailed to America and were married in Richfield, Utah, in 1875. Rebecca was the tenth of 14 children born to Ole and Julia.

While Rebecca was a small child, she developed a great love for the missionaries. She delighted in the missionary stories she heard at her mother's knee during the early years of her life.

Rebecca silently wished she could someday have missionaries come to her home like her mother had had. "I couldn't know then," she said, "but I would have more missionaries come to my home than anyone else in the church."[27]

Rebecca was blessed with many spiritual experiences while living in the Joseph Smith home. When moved to do so, she would relate a particular incident that was especially sacred to her. She referred to it as the most wonderful experience she had while living in Palmyra.

"It was a hot summer day, and we had had a lot of visitors that day. It had been a hard day for me. I had a baby just a year old, and I had carried him around on my arm most of the day to get my work done. I was too warm. Everything had gone against us. Night time came and we had had lunch for our visitors and supper at night and I had put my

26. Ibid.
27. Ibid.

children to bed. We had a very nice evening with house-work all done.

"Dr. Talmage and some missionaries were there, and we had a wonderful evening talking together. They all seemed tired, so I took them upstairs and showed them where they could sleep.

"When I came down, I decided to pick up a few things and make things easier for myself in the morning. But I was so weary and so tired that I was crying a little as I straight-ened things around. Everybody was in bed and asleep but me. I looked at the clock and it was 11:00, and I can remem-ber so well that I said, 'I better call it a day.'

"I went into my room and my husband and my baby were sound asleep. It was peaceful and quiet. I got myself ready for bed, and I was crying on my pillow. Then this dream or vision came to me.

"I thought it was another day. It had been a wonderful morning. I had prepared breakfast for my visitors. My chil-dren were happily playing around. I had done my work and cared for the baby, and he was contented and happy. Then I prepared lunch. I called our visitors in to lunch, and we were all seated around the table. My little baby was in his high chair, and everything was just peaceful and wonderful and sweet.

"There was a knock at the front door. I went in and opened it, and there was a very handsome young man standing there. I just took it for granted that he was just another new missionary that had come to see us. I said, 'You're here just in time for lunch. Come with me.'

"As he walked through the little hall into the dining room, I noticed he put some pamphlets down on the little table there. We walked into the dining room, and I introduced him around and then I said, 'Now, you sit right here by Dr. Talmage, and I'll set a plate for you.'

"I thought, of course, that he was strange to all of us, and yet he and Dr. Talmage seemed so happy to see each other. They talked about such wonderful things while we were eating. Some of them we could hardly understand. The spirit and mood present there was so peaceful and nice, and everyone seemed so happy to be together.

"After the meal was over, Dr. Talmage said to the missionary, 'Now, let's go outside and just be alone and enjoy the spirit of this wonderful place because,' he said, 'you'll soon have to leave.'

"I put my baby to bed and the other little ones went out to play, and then I was alone with this young man. He thanked me for having him to dinner and told me how much it meant for him to be there. He told me that he thought that the children were so sweet and well trained, and I felt so happy about that.

"And then we walked in the hall together, and he said, 'I have far to go so I must be on my way.'

"I turned from him for just a moment to pick up the little pamphlets that he had put on the table; and when I turned back to him it was the Savior who stood before me, and He was in His glory. I could not tell you the love and the sweetness that He had in His face and in His eyes. Lovingly He laid His hands on my shoulders, and He looked down into my face with the kindest face that I have ever seen. And this is what He said to me:

"'Sister Bean, this day hasn't been too hard for you, has it?'

"I said, 'Oh, no, I have been so happy with my work and everything has gone so well.'

"Then He said, 'I promise you if you will go about your work every day as you have done it this day, you will be equal to it. Remember these missionaries represent me on this earth and all you do unto them, you do unto me.'

"And I know I was crying as we walked through the hall out onto the porch. He repeated the same thing: 'These missionaries represent me on earth, and all that you do unto them, you do unto me.'

"Then He started upward. The roof of the porch was no obstruction for Him to go through nor for me to see through. He went upward and upward and upward. I wondered and wondered how I could see Him so far away. And then all at once He disappeared, and I was crying on my pillow like I was when I went to bed."[28]

Rebecca bore humble testimony many times that never again was there any frustration in her soul. "Never again did too many missionaries come that I couldn't find beds for them to sleep in or enough food to give them," she said. "And the great love that I had for missionaries even then became greater after what the Savior had said to me. And how I wish that every missionary that went out into the world could feel that His love and His guidance was only a prayer away. They're preaching His gospel and how much they mean to Him. And all the years I lived there I felt the love, as did all my family, the love and influence of the Prophet Joseph Smith and the love and influence of the Savior. I believe that if I could live well enough in this life that I could meet the Prophet Joseph when I go beyond, I believe he would know me and I would know him. And there will be a friendship deep between us few earthly friends have known."[29]

---

28. Ibid.
29. Ibid.

A Library Victory

Palmyra had a fine library for a small town. While perusing the bookshelves one afternoon, Willard became aware that they had a long shelf full of anti-Mormon books and nothing official in the church's favor. He drew this to the attention of the librarian and asked permission to put some Mormon literature on their shelves, emphasizing the fact that the first edition of the Book of Mormon was printed in their fair city. The librarian promised to take it up with the Board of Directors, Kings Daughters, and let him know their decision.

An old maid daughter of one of the most popular pioneer ministers who had helped to make early history in the village was at the head of the Kings Daughters organization. She had taught school for over forty years and quite naturally had an interest in the welfare of the young people. She flatly refused to even consider the possibility of allowing Mormon reading matter on the library shelves. She told them that the object of Mormons everywhere was to "sow the seeds of their diabolical religion among the young people," etc.[30]

Many years passed, and the president of the Kings Daughters died. Willard received a letter from the new president which read:

"Some time ago you asked for the privilege of putting a Book of Mormon and other reading matter in our library. The way has now been cleared by death of the opposition, and your literature will be gladly received."[31]

They went even further by ordering the librarian to place no book that even mentioned Mormons on their shelves before having Mr. Bean pass on it. "We want no literature on our shelves that is offensive to the Mormons," they insisted.[32]

30. Bean, Autobiography, p. 107.
31. Ibid., p. 113.
32. Ibid.

Acquisition of the Hill Cumorah

Willard's assignments from the First Presidency of the Church were not limited to making friends and converts. In addition, he was to arrange for the purchase, whenever possible, of Church historical properties in and around Palmyra. Pliny Sexton owned the Hill Cumorah (or Drumlin Hill as it was then called), and Willard was especially anxious to get that piece of property into the hands of the Church.

The Bean's first experience on the Hill Cumorah had not been a pleasant one. After being in Palmyra for only a few days, Willard and Rebecca drove their horse and buggy to the hill with the intention of walking to the top and enjoying the sacred grounds. They were met by a man with a shotgun.

"No one steps on this hill that belongs to the Mormon Church," he bellowed.

"Do you own it?" asked Willard.

"No, but I work here," the man insisted, "and you can't go up there."[33]

Willard and his wife climbed aboard their buggy and returned home deeming it advisable to wait for more pleasant circumstances.

President Heber J. Grant went to Palmyra several years later to check on the possibilities of acquiring the hill. President Grant and his counselor, C. W. Nibley, accompanied Willard to visit with Pliny Sexton at his bank. The owner suggested a price of $100,000 for the purchase of the hill. Willard jokingly accused the ambitious banker of "listening tell of the fabulous wealth of the Mormon Church"[34] and informed him that the Church had done quite well without the hill for nearly a hundred years and would continue to do so until a more realistic offer was made.

---

33. Bean tape recording.
34. Bean, Autobiography, p. 115.

President Nibley was non-communicative as they drove back to the farm. Finally he confided, "When the Lord wants us to get possession of that hill, the way will be opened up."[35]

And opened up it was. Mr. Sexton died, and his estate fell into the hands of distant nieces who pledged never to sell to the Mormons at any price. One by one, the nieces passed away. The lawyer of the Sexton estate, Mr. C. C. Congdon, called Willard to his office one afternoon in late February 1928 and announced that an opportune time had come to make arrangements for the purchase of the hill.

In the final analysis, Willard purchased the Hill Cumorah, three farms bordering the hill, and Grange Hall, a building which made a fine chapel for the saints, all for $53,000. There was over 600 acres of land. The buildings alone were worth $10,000. The final purchase was made for a fraction of the original asking price.

Willard's letter to the First Presidency crossed in the mail with a telegram from Salt Lake saying:

"See lawyer of Sexton estate and get definite offer for Hill Cumorah alone if possible, if not with adjacent properties. Put it in writing and put up forfeit and let us hear from you at earliest convenience."[36]

The telegram was signed by each member of the First Presidency—President Heber J. Grant, A. W. Ivins and C. W. Nibley. Willard observed that the telegram was dated the same day he had written to them, and it requested that he do something he had just done in every detail.

The following day Willard received another telegram as follows:

"Terms satisfactory. Close deal."[37]

---

35. Ibid.
36. Ibid., p. 117.
37. Ibid.

CHURCH OF JESUS CHRIST OF LATTER-DAY SAINTS
OFFICE OF THE PRESIDING BISHOPRIC
SALT LAKE CITY, UTAH.

September 23, 1924.

Elder Willard Bean,

Palymra Farm.

Dear Brother:

Your interesting letter was received and we read it to the Presidency at our meeting yesterday.

We were asked to have you keep us posted in respect to the matter of the Hill Cumorah, and advise us of any developments in connection therewith, but we should not appear too anxious about it. If we use caution and the Lord wants us to have possession of the Hill, it will be so over-ruled. Or, on the other hand, no matter how anxious and how hard we may try, unless the matter is over-ruled in our favor, we will not succeed.

We are always glad to hear from you. Hope you will write often and keep us advised as to the progress of the work under your direction.

Your brethren in the Gospel,

THE PRESIDING BISHOPRIC,

By _cwnibley_

CWN/LA.

February 2, 1928.

Elder Willard Bean,

     Palmyra, N.Y.

Dear Brother Bean:

     Please secure a definite offer in writing
if you can possibly do so, from the executors of Mr.
Sexton's estate, for the Hill farm of 170 acres. If
they will not sell it alone, get a definite offer on
the other pieces of property with the hill.

     But to make it binding it would be best to
have this offer in writing. If you have to pay ten or
twenty dollars to secure a thirty day option, this
would be the safest way to hold it.

     An early reply will oblige,

     Sincerely your brethren,

First Presidency.

CHURCH OF JESUS CHRIST OF LATTER DAY SAINTS
OFFICE OF THE FIRST PRESIDENCY
SALT LAKE CITY, UTAH

2

                                        March 6th, 1928.

Elder Willard W. Bean,
Joseph Smith Farm,
Palmyra, N.Y.

Dear Brother Bean:

        We have read your letter of February 27th
with a great deal of interest.

        We were very glad to learn that you had
secured an option on the Hill Cumorah Farm and other
property before receiving word from us to do so. We
had already noticed the singular coincidence of your
writing to us the very same day and possibly the same hour
that we were writing to you.

        The Presiding Bishopric, so we understand,
have invited you to come to Conference, and we will
be very glad to see you at that time and confer with
you relative to our interests in that part of the
country.

        Congratulating you on the final consummation
of this deal and in such a satisfactory way, we are,

                    Sincerely your brethren,

                                        First Presidency.

February 11, 1931.

Elder Willard W. Bean,
c/o Joseph Smith Farm,
Palmyra, New York.

Dear Brother Bean:

Your letter of January 5th came duly to hand.

We certainly appreciate the fact that the building at Palmyra, for which we gave $6000.00, has been experted by an insurance company engineer as being worth $38,000.00, with a depreciation of only $6000.00, making a net of $32,000., or five times what we paid for it.

We do not think that you should insure the property for more than $15,000, because we believe that is about all you could burn out of the building if you were to have a fire.

Pleased to hear that religious work in your branch is progressing nicely. Actual faith in Jesus Christ apparently does not seem to be very popular even with religious people at the present time. The Gospel has a big task on itself in leavening the lump, from ministers down.

We turned your manuscript over to Brother Talmage and he returned it to us a day or two ago. We enclose herewith his letter of comment. The manuscript will be returned to you under separate cover. We are so busy that we did not have time to read the manuscript ourselves.

With all good wishes,

Sincerely your brethren,

Enc.

Willard reflected on President Nibley's words when he said, "When the Lord wants us to get possession of that hill, the way will be opened up." No wonder President Grant remarked at General Conference in the Tabernacle, "We have recently come into possession of the Hill Cumorah, and it looks very much like it came about providentially."[38]

In the ensuing years, Willard was instrumental in acquiring the Martin Harris and Peter Whitmer farms. He was responsible for reforesting the Hill Cumorah in an effort to restore it to the natural beauty that existed there when the prophet received the gold plates. Willard, assisted by his three sons, a brother, Virginius, local missionaries and hired hands, planted 65,000 little evergreen trees in addition to 3,000 small hardwood trees—the latter being dug up from the outskirts of the Sacred Grove. Today a mighty forest has grown on that picturesque church landmark.

The Angel Moroni Monument

After purchasing the Hill Cumorah and reforesting it, the Bean's had a roadway built up the hill, an information bureau constructed at the bottom of the hill, and a monument erected on top.

When Norwegian-born sculptor, Torlief S. Knaphus, learned that the church had purchased the hill, he envisioned a monument standing at the top. He imagined the Angel Moroni standing stately at its peak.

With pencil and pad, Torlief began sketching. After completing seven possible designs, he went to Ensign Peak, all alone in the darkness of night, and laid them out on the ground. Kneeling in prayer, he asked forgiveness if he had done wrong by pursuing his desire. He prayed that he might know which one of his sketches was the one to be used—if, indeed, any of them were. He prayed to know which one he should take to the church authorities or whether it was proper for him to go to the church leaders at all.

---

38. Ibid.

When he opened his eyes, a light shone all around him. He could see clearly all seven drawings spread on the ground before him. A finger pointed to the one that he himself thought was best, and he heard a voice say, "This is the one."

"How will I approach the authorities?" Torlief asked out loud. "What will they think? Have I done right to do this?"[39]

The voice told him to go to the church office building the following morning, and he would find the brethren waiting for him.

Torlief went to the office the next day as he had been told. It was as though it had been planned. The church authorities greeted him as if they had sent for him. He carefully laid the drawings out on the table. The brethren looked them over and they, too, selected the one the night visitor had pointed to.

Torlief stayed with the Beans at the time the monument was placed on the Hill Cumorah. He related the story of its inception to them.

"Was it the Angel Moroni that came to you, Brother Knaphus?" Rebecca asked after hearing the story.

His answer was simple. "Sister Bean," he smiled, "that's my secret."[40]

There was a great celebration and conference in connection with the placing of the

Angel Moroni Monument on the Hill Cumorah. Willard laid the wreath at the foot of the monument, and there was rejoicing by all present on that momentous occasion.

The Organization of the First Branch

Eventually enough converts were made to warrant renting a hall and organizing a branch of the church. In 1925 the first Re-

---

39. Bean tape recording.
40. Ibid.

lief Society in Palmyra was organized. Rebecca served as its first president. A year later the first branch and Sunday School were organized followed by Mutual Improvement Association, Gleaner Girls and Boy Scouts.

There was a great need for assistance in Palmyra at that time, and Rebecca became an assistant to the county poormaster. He relied on her more than he did his own organization to help get layettes for young mothers and fill other community needs. Rebecca had been trained well as a member of the Church, and she was prepared to take care of others as well as her own family.

In 1926 the first branch of The Church of Jesus Christ of Latter-day Saints was fully organized. It boasted a membership of three families.

As membership grew and visitors and conferences became more frequent, church meetings were held in the Sacred Grove. People sat on chairs, logs, benches, planks—anything available that would accommodate one or two hundred people. Testimony meetings in the Grove often lasted most of the day.

When the sacrament was passed, a large loaf of bread would be broken into about three pieces and passed down each row. People broke off their own little piece of bread and handed the chunk to the next person. The water was passed in full glasses with each person taking a sip of water as it was passed down the row.

In 1960, 34 years after the organization of an LDS branch, the first chapel was built in Joseph Smith's home town.

The First Pageant

Norma Fairbanks, one of the lady missionaries in Palmyra, wrote what was to be the forerunner of the Hill Cumorah Pageant. This maiden performance was staged in the Sacred Grove in 1926. The Beans had three children at this time. Eight-year-old Alvin was asked to play the part of the Prophet Joseph Smith.

When offered the part, Alvin replied, "Well, I'll have to think about it."

"Why?" everyone asked.

"I'll just have to think about that," he insisted.[41]

It was B. H. Roberts of The First Quorum of Seventy (and Alvin's favorite visitor) who prevailed upon him to participate. Finally agreeing, Alvin said, "Well, OK. I'll take the part of Joseph Smith if I don't have to see an angel."[42]

That possibility had been worrying the young lad. He didn't know how he would react if an angel actually appeared.

The Greatest Musician of All Time

A young missionary came to Palmyra just as the Beans were preparing to return to Utah. Two of his brothers had spent time with the family in Palmyra.

The new missionary was an outstanding musician. At his father's request, he had a special blessing prior to departing on his mission. His blessing revealed: "You shall be the greatest musician of all time."[43]

Following his service in the mission field, this young man worked with choral groups but felt a desire to go back to college and get more formal education in music. He married an attractive and supportive young woman, and they made their plans to continue his musical pursuits.

He worked and studied in several eastern cities and accepted a job back east after graduation. He was a successful husband and father when he was suddenly stricken with polio. He was paralyzed from the neck down.

41. Ibid.
42. Alvin Bean transcript, p. 24.
43. Bean tape recording.

Friends in his Salt Lake City ward fasted and prayed for him. He was administered to. His father went quickly to New York, fasting and praying all the way. Elders went to the hospital and administered to the young man again. Great faith was exercised, and the priesthood was strong—yet that night, the boy died.

His death was a shock to his family and friends. His father was a mission president in California at the time of his son's passing. After the funeral, the father went down to the beach where he walked on the sand and talked out loud to the Lord. He pleaded with his Heavenly Father for understanding as to why his son, with such a future before him, had to be taken. Wasn't his faith strong enough? Was he at fault? What was wrong?

Then, in the distance coming towards him, he saw someone—a white figure. As the person neared, he could see it was the Savior, and He was in His glory.

The Savior said to him, "Sorrow no more for it was necessary for your son to be taken. He is now writing the music that will be played when I come to rule and reign upon this earth."[44]

Leaving Palmyra

With only a faint echo of the original persecution still surviving in Palmyra, Willard and Rebecca Bean and their children became well accepted in the city. They were invited to join the Parent-Teacher Organization. Willard was selected to be on the Board of Control, became a charter member of the Palmyra Lion's Club and served as president of that organization. He became a scout committeeman for Wayne County, an officer in the Civic and Businessmen's Organization, and a member of the Rochester Chamber of Commerce. He was invited to give many talks before business and civic organizations.

Rebecca was president of the first Relief Society in Palmyra. She had the respect and admiration of all who knew her. Local charita-

---

44. Ibid.

ble organizations cooperated with her and would furnish any materials the Church needed including entire bolts of yardage. The Kings Daughters who had been so prejudiced became friendly.

The Bean children excelled in all areas. Phyllis, Willard's daughter by his first wife, Gussie Dee Felts, won the spelling contest in Ontario County. Palmyra was valedictorian of her class in elementary school as well as in high school. When Alvin was in the seventh grade, he was selected to represent Wayne County in the spelling contest at the State Fair in Syracuse. Dawn was honored as valedictorian of his high school class. In a musical vein, Palmyra was an accomplished pianist, Dawn outstanding on the clarinet, and Alvin and Kelvin proficient on the trap drums.

Willard staged benefit plays in the high school auditorium and local opera house. Church-sponsored plays and pageants were performed in the Sacred Grove, and soon Eastern States Mission Conferences were held there and atop the Hill Cumorah.

On many occasions, Rebecca and Willard paid their way to public banquets and gatherings only to be escorted to the minister's table with the announcement: "This is where you belong. Your tickets are on your plates."[45]

Willard and Rebecca were sent to Palmyra for five years or more. It was principally more. They were well into their 25th year before receiving their release from their mission on the farm. It had been a great satisfaction to them to see the sentiment change from sub-zero to absolute respect and admiration.

When they received their release and prepared to return to Salt Lake City, the family intended to keep it a secret until they were ready to leave. Word slipped out, however, and the townspeople, not realizing the temporary nature of mission calls, had accepted them as a permanent and respected part of the community and were as loath to see them go as the Beans were to leave. Many

---

45. Bean, Autobiography, p. 119.

stopped them on the street to express their disappointment at the prospects of losing them.

"We want you to know that the news that you are soon to leave us came as a shock," one gentleman said, "and we think the Mormon Church is making a big mistake in taking you away from here."[46]

Several local ministers called Willard to express their deep feelings about their departure. "We most certainly hate to see you leave Palmyra," said one minister. "You always bring a ray of sunshine into our gatherings, and our associations have been so pleasant that we are a little apprehensive lest they send another man who may not fit into the gap that will surely result by your leaving."[47]

The Lion's Club honored them with a formal banquet and entertainment. The Master of Ceremonies paid them this glowing compliment:

> "We are doing honor to a family that came to Palmyra some years ago. When they settled on the Joseph Smith Farm, some of our super-pious citizens started a tirade with the object of getting rid of them. But as they proved themselves good citizens, we soon learned to tolerate them, then we learned to admire and respect them, and now we love them. It is with reluctance that we now bid farewell to the most versatile family that ever lived in Wayne County."[48]

The Beans were also honored by the villagers and country folk who said, "We are not all members of civic organizations, but we are all friends to the Bean family."[49]

As Willard delivered his farewell address at a banquet given by his friends, many of them wept like children. Rebecca had endeared herself to them as well, and they all loved her.

---

46. Ibid., p. 120.
47. Ibid.
48. Ibid.
49. Ibid.

The party went on far into the evening; and as they bid each other goodbye, many eyes were wet with tears. The Beans had truly captured the hearts of the people in Palmyra—a city which had been described to them as the most prejudiced city in the world when they were asked to accept the mission call more than 24 years earlier.

 B. H. Roberts with Alvin at 24th of July mission conference in the Sacred Grove. Tents (in background) were set up for meetings (1926)

President Heber J. Grant conducting Missionary Conference on the Hill Cumorah (approximately 1935)

Joseph Smith Home in Palmyra, New York (about 1930)

Alvin and Dawn feeding chickens (July 1930)

Parlor of the Smith home. The table in the middle of the room was built by Brigham Young. Part of the Book of Mormon was translated in this room.

Hill Cumorah (circa 1925)

Kelvin, Palmyra, Alvin ad Dawn with family dog (1925)

The Angel Moroni Monument was placed on top of the Hill Cumorah under the direction of Willard Bean.

President Heber J. Grant carries Dawn; Alvin and Palmyra stand by (1920)

Alvin and Rebecca feeding African geese across the street from the Smith home

Willard flanked by his sons in 1947.
Kelvin, Alvin, Paul and Dawn

Willard and Rebecca with Alvin and
Palmyra in side yard of Smith home

Missionaries stand by creek where
baptisms were performed in Joseph
Smith's time as well as at the time
the Beans lived there (1930)

Rebecca Peterson Bean

Willard Washington Bean

Alvin Bean

Kelvin Bean

Palmyra Bean

Dawn Bean

Alvin and Dawn feeding
chickens (July 1930)

Bean family: Willard in back.
Rebecca holding Kelvin,
Palmyra, Alvin and Dawn.

Hill Cumorah (1920s)

Willard was born in this home in Provo, Utah, in 1868.

EARTH LIFE DRAWS TO A CLOSE

As Willard neared the end of his life, he wrote these words in a Salt Lake City newspaper:

"I am now within sight of the 80 oneth mile post of my checkered career, which has been very variegated. It used to be Kid Bean; next it was Willard Bean; then Mr. Bean; and in some places, Brother Bean; then the Fighting Parson; now Old Man Bean; and yet a little longer my friends who call to see me will say, well—'he looks natural'; and then... well, I'll just take my place along with the long line of forgotten men."

Willard died in his home at 112 Duplex Place just half a block from Temple Square in Salt Lake City, Utah, on September 25, 1949. He was one of thirty children—his father, Judge George Washington Bean of the Superior Court of Utah, having married three wives under the old law of polygamy. Every one of the children born of these marriages was physically and mentally above average. His father was an old frontiersman and Indian fighter of powerful physique and strong intellect. Willard, in turn, was an earnest advocate of physical culture and moral purity.

At the age of 16, Willard accompanied the presiding bishopric as they traveled to visit the saints and avoid those who would have imprisoned them for polygamy. At 18 he was an ordinance worker in the Manti Temple. When he was 22, he served a full-time mission in the Southern States under the direction of President J. Golden Kimball.

Following his mission, Willard attended Brigham Young Academy before serving as a physical education instructor at the University of Utah for two years. He studied physical education and naturopathy in San Francisco, California, then returned to Salt Lake City where he leased a sanitarium, started a gym and taught boxing.

Willard was a member of the Salt Lake City and Richfield, Utah, police forces and editor of the Richfield Reaper newspaper. He was active in civic affairs. He served a 24½-year mission for The Church of Jesus Christ of Latter-day Saints on the Joseph Smith Farm in Palmyra, New York. While there he authored two books, *Gospel Conversations* and *ABC History of Palmyra and the Beginning of Mormonism*. He also co-authored the book, *Geography of the Book of Mormon* with E. Cecil McGavin.

After being released from his mission in Palmyra, Willard served for ten years as a missionary on Temple Square in Salt Lake City.

"I'll just take my place along with the long line of forgotten men" could never be the lot of Willard Bean. A man of such magnificent character could never be forgotten. One who has contributed so greatly to society as well as to the church should be remembered not only by his family but by all who love life, their country, and their Heavenly Father.

Rebecca lived alone for 27 years after the death of her husband. She was always quick to emphasize that even though she lived alone, she was never lonely. She said:

"My days and nights in the sunset of my life are sweet and peaceful and filled with golden memories. I have such love for all the missionaries I have known. I was 'mom' to thousands of missionaries, and I could never live long enough to thank my Father in Heaven for all the blessings that I have had in my life and that are mine today."

Rebecca Bean was truly one of the choice daughters of our Heavenly Father. She was an influence for good in the lives of all she met and made each day brighter for so many people as they visited with her. She was especially kind and compassionate to the elderly and handicapped who came daily to visit with her in her home near Temple Square. Rebecca passed away in Orem, Utah, on June 25, 1976.

Many lives have been touched and will yet be touched in the eternities by this remarkable couple, Willard and Rebecca Bean.

A LETTER TO HER CHILDREN

(Rebecca Bean wrote this letter to her children in 1953, 23 years before her death. Her children were instructed not to open it until she passed away.)

August 26, 1953

My dearest children,

When you read this I will be gone. But there must be no sorrow. Death has to come as well as birth. I hope my love and my influence will be round about you as long as you live.

Remember always this life is only a preparation for the life to come, so live it well and be proud of your heritage. Gain a strong testimony of the gospel and do not fail to get your temple work done.

I have loved you deeply with the love that only mothers know. I haven't much to leave you except my love and a testimony that is humble and sincere. The Prophet Joseph is as real to me as any living person I have ever known, and there will be a friendship deep between us few earthly friends have known.

My testimony of the Savior is sacred and glorious for I have seen Him, heard His voice and felt the touch of His hand. Life has been good to me—better than I have ever deserved.

Be kind and helpful to each other, and love one another as I have loved you. Until we meet again, my love everlasting.

Your devoted Mother

SOURCES

Willard Washington Bean Autobiography in possession of Vicki Bean Topliff, 66 North 340 West, Orem, Utah 84057.

Willard Bean Scrapbook in possession of Barton Pliny Bean, 12 Pt. Loma, Corona del Mar, California 92625. Also on microfilm in Brigham Young University Library, Provo, Utah.

Rebecca P. Bean talk to fireside group in Salt Lake City, Utah, in October 1964. Tape recording and transcript in possession of Vicki Bean Topliff.

Alvin Pliny Bean fireside address in Huntington Beach, California, on November 5, 1978. Tape recording and transcript in possession of Vicki Bean Topliff.

Alvin Pliny Bean talk entitled, "Willard Washington Bean, Mission in Tennessee 1892-1894." Transcript in possession of Vicki Bean Topliff.

George Washington Bean Autobiography and Family Record by Flora Bean Horne, copyright 1945, in possession of Vicki Bean Topliff.

Genealogical records and Family Group Sheets.

About the Author

V icki Bean Topliff is the daughter of Willard and Rebecca Bean's second child, Alvin. From the time she was small she heard stories about "life on the farm" and longed to go there and experience it with her father.

It wasn't until 1973, when she was 30 years old, that she had the privilege of flying to Palmyra, New York, with her father and spending three days visiting his home town. She learned then that the Bean name would forever be sounded for good in that community. The welcome mat was out and the doors were open wide for members of the Bean family.

In 1988 Vicki married Edward Robert Topliff who had joined the Church in October 1987. Since Ed had been a member less than a year, they were unable to be sealed in the temple on their scheduled wedding date. In their eagerness to be married in a meaningful location, they requested permission to hold the ceremony in the Joseph Smith Home. Due to Vicki's heritage and the impact the Bean family had had on the town of Palmyra, permission was granted. Accompanied by Alvin and Dorothy Bean, Vicki and Ed were married in that sacred place on June 7, 1988. Missionary couples from surrounding Church Historical Sites gathered in the small living room that afternoon to witness the event. Walking across the street to the Sacred Grove after the ceremony, Alvin told stories about his life in Palmyra in the early 1900's. Not a dry eye was found in that group as spiritual experiences were shared. Vicki has seven children and 25 grandchildren. She and Ed lived in Orem, Utah, until her passing from a rare and untreatable cancer on August 3, 2014.